George Ward Nichols

The Sanctuary

A story of the civil war

George Ward Nichols

The Sanctuary
A story of the civil war

ISBN/EAN: 9783337224288

Printed in Europe, USA, Canada, Australia, Japan

Cover: Foto ©ninafisch / pixelio.de

More available books at **www.hansebooks.com**

"There was a pleading earnestness in his eyes which caused Agnes to tremble with uncontrollable emotion, and she covered her face with her hands, and would have fled from him." [Page 134.

THE SANCTUARY:

A STORY OF THE CIVIL WAR.

BY

GEORGE WARD NICHOLS,

AUTHOR OF "THE STORY OF THE GREAT MARCH."

With Illustrations.

NEW YORK:
HARPER & BROTHERS, PUBLISHERS,
FRANKLIN SQUARE.
1866.

Entered, according to Act of Congress, in the year one thousand eight hundred and sixty-six, by

HARPER & BROTHERS,

In the Clerk's Office of the District Court of the Southern District of New York.

PREFACE.

IT was my good fortune, several years ago, to visit the Old World. While crossing the English Channel upon my journey toward home, my mind impressed with the glory of splendid architecture and beautiful pictures, I saw a ship under full sail, with our national banner flying at the mast-head. While the vision thrilled me with emotions of pride and exultation, which all the wonders of European art had failed to inspire, yet there was mingled with them a sense of humiliation at the thought that it floated over four millions of human beings in slavery.

During the years of our Civil War, it has been my duty to make longer journeys in my native land, not, as in Europe years ago, a spectator merely, but as an actor in scenes where the beautiful, the heroic, and the terrible were strangely mingled. Day after day I saw the symbol of our national unity outspread by a thousand patriot hands, or when tossing amid the fray of battle, I have watched its surge as token of victory; and grander than all, as crowds of refugees, white and black, sought its folds for protection and liberty, I no longer felt humiliated nor ashamed, for the flag of our union symbolized to me, as it must to all the world, Liberty, in its widest, purest, noblest meaning.

I was impressed by this thought more than by any other during my experiences in the war, and the story herein narrated, which is founded upon incidents within my own knowledge, has suggested to me the title of

The Sanctuary.

ILLUSTRATIONS.

	PAGE
SCENE AT BONAVENTURA	*Frontispiece*
THE OLD SLAVE	149
ZIMRI AND CHARLOTTE	178
ZIMRI'S REVENGE	188
HORTON AND KATE	254
DALTON AND AGNES	280

THE SANCTUARY.

I.

N the fall of 1864, a detachment of the Federal Army in pursuit of Hood was encamped on a plantation near the entrance to a pass in the mountains of Northern Alabama. By one of those chances incident to a marching army, officers and men, separated from their transportation wagons, had gone into bivouac, and were making such preparations for the night's rest as their perseverance and energy could secure.

The immediate locality from which this story commences was a huge camp-fire, made from logs and rails, which crackled, and sizzled, and roared as the gathering flames were swayed about by the fitful wind, which, governed apparently by no regular laws, came moaning from the forest and hill-sides, shifting this way and then that, the whirling volumes of flame and smoke giving little comfort and less rest to the party of officers grouped about, who, hungry and tired, were making the most of their poor circumstances. Off in the deep gorge could be heard the click and thug of many axes in the hands of pioneers, striving to remove the obstructions which the retreating army had interposed by felling thousands of trees across the single wagon-road, in hope of checking the swift pursuit. In the valley below, and on the slopes of the hills, which, upon all sides but one, formed an amphitheatre, were many other gleaming camp-fires, and far above, from a jutting mountain cliff, the torches from a signal-station were waving rapidly to and fro, sending messages across the intervening hills to some distant correspondent miles away with the extreme advance of the army. The sky, which had been so clear at sunset, was now darkened by swiftly drifting masses of clouds, and in a spiteful, threatening way, a few scattered rain-drops —the skirmishers from advancing columns of storm —sputtered in the desolate camp-fires.

Near our special camp-fire—for the gathering darkness now shuts us in to the group with which our story is concerned—was a log hut, and attached to the fruit-trees about it, to the fences, and to stakes driven into the ground, were the horses of the party, more contented than their masters in the enjoyment of the bountiful supplies of forage and grain which were found upon the place. Around the fire the officers were grouped in attitudes more picturesque than comfortable. One, the luckiest of all, had secured possession of a large feed-trough, into which he had thrust himself bodily. Another had obtained a claim in fee-simple to a bee-hive which had that day been rifled of its inhabitants and sweets, and whose present tenant adhered to his property more closely than he at the moment was aware. Others sat or were stretched upon rails, while others still lay upon the bare ground, first offering one portion and then another of their bodies to the grateful warmth of the fire.

Taken at the best, the time, place, and circumstances were not especially calculated to enamour a neophyte with a soldier's life. But there were few of these men who had not gone through with half a dozen hard campaigns, and they had many a remembered glory, recent or remote, of victories won from the very skirts of defeat, of the overmastering siege, or of charges that defied death, to balance against their immediate discomfort. After all, it was not so much the glories of the battle-field that were recalled as a compensation for their present dreary situation, but rather, by that curious eccentricity of human nature which leads men in their miseries, in a kind of malicious self-torture, to draw vivid images of delights beyond their reach, they set over against the hardships of the camp the delicious comforts of a distant home, or the refinements of civilized life, from which they had been so long divorced.

"How I would like," said Captain Oakland, from his huge feed-trough, "to crawl between the clean sheets of a bed that I know of in that dear old home of mine in New York."

"A bed is a charming institution on a night like this," replied Major Cramer, who had not asked for leave of absence during four years of service, and who had left a wife and two little ones in a quiet home in Ohio. "Yes," he continued, as he pushed into the fire a half-burned rail, which every moment threatened to roll over upon an unconscious, half-asleep comrade, "Oakland's wish includes many other comforts the opposite of the present situation. A grate-fire, dressing-gown, the evening paper, babies, and all that; but at this moment there is a gnawing sensation at the stomach, which induces me to believe that, next to 'standing in the deadly breach,' the highest aspiration of the soldier is to eat!"

"Eat!" shouted Leveridge, a corps inspector of unusual height, whose slender body, buttoned close into a forage-jacket, and whose thin legs, tightly incased in high Wellington boots, were in comical contrast with a huge mustache that overhung an extensive mouth, which suggested extraordinary capacities for mastication. "I imagine myself seated at one of those neat little tables at the Maison Dorée, with that blessed old Martini proposing gombo-soup, poulet a l'Espagnol, with all the *entremets*, jelly, and a bottle of Beaune or Burgundy—"

"Stop there! That'll do!" was the cry from several suffering listeners. "I'll compromise for a piece of hard tack and a cup of coffee," said Cramer. "Halloo, here's Horton!" as a young man dismounted from a horse which showed signs of having been hard ridden. "Well, Horton, where have you been all day, and where are our wagons? The last question first."

"The wagons are a good mile back, and I don't know how many trees are to be chopped up before they can arrive at this point. They'll be here by morning, no doubt, if there's any satisfaction in that. As to your other question, it would be easier to tell where I have *not* been. You know the Fifteenth Corps got on the wrong road this morning, and I had to go back and steer them right. Has there been any fighting?"

"No. Hood made a twenty-five mile march of it yesterday, and passed this paradise just in time to save himself."

Rest—such as the soldier has under the roughest of circumstances—had for some time settled down upon our encampment, when the sentinel, who, wrapped in his overcoat, had been pacing his beat across the entrance to the road, called out,

"Halt! who comes there?"

"Officers and guard with prisoners from the front," was the reply which came from a group of men thus suddenly brought to a stand in the deep shadow. A few words passed between the sentinel and the guard, and the party emerged from the shadow into the glare of the fire-light, and then plunged into the darkness again. An officer, wearing the insignia of a major of artillery, who, during the evening, had been lying upon the ground, gazing with a preoccupied air into the fire, and who had apparently paid little heed to any thing which had been going on thus far, and who had sprung to his feet at the reply to the sentinel's challenge, followed rapidly the steps of the squad of prisoners as they disappeared over the brow of the hill.

"There goes Major Dalton again upon his almost hopeless search after his lost brother," murmured Horton, as he composed himself for the brief interval of slumber yet left him before daybreak.

Still on the mountain's crest the flaming signal torches told their mysterious story to their distant correspondents, and the sound of the axes could still be heard in the forest as the watchful sentinel paced back and forth.

II.

A TALL young man of twenty-three, who, being the son of a prosperous merchant in the city of Savannah, had known little of the sharp conflict of life; whose gentle face disclosed, in a large measure, the spirit of the beautiful, and gave prophetic signals of a possible heroism upon which, as yet, no call had been made, and whose soft dark blue eyes seemed rather to reflect the flowery savannas of his native South than to give token of the stern Saxon strength that really lurked in their hidden depths—such was the David Dalton of our story in the month of April, 1861, when the evil star of Rebellion rose and stood defiant above dismantled Fort Sumter, in Charleston Harbor.

A young woman of eighteen years, in this self-same evil hour, who seemed almost a child—for the storm that was hurtling in the air above her had not yet revealed the might of her womanhood—with hazel eyes, solemn, reflective, and as subtle and serene as the sea, with a face that showed a capacity for passion equaled only by its capacity for sorrow —this was Agnes Saumur, toward whom the heart of Dalton had been drifting for years.

To both these the South, and the possible destiny of the South, was ineffably dear; it was to them both an inspiration, a rapturous dream. But in this revolutionary crisis they differed widely in their estimate of the situation, according to the difference of their education and intimate personal associations, and according to the difference which there always is between a man's judgment of events and a woman's. In the attempt on the part of the national government to command the allegiance of Southern citizens she could see only a tyrannical aggression. He saw at the root of secession a despotism as bitter and relentless as any of which history holds a record. He knew that his father, and many other citizens of Savannah, though in ordinary times they wielded that moral influence which always accompanies respectability and honesty, were surrounded by a wall of hatred. He knew that the time had already come when the diabolic spirit which had been hitherto under restraint would break through all barriers and become a consuming fire. He saw the wolves even under their sheep's clothing. His great anxiety was for his family. They must, at any hazard, be removed to a haven of security, where the coming strife could not reach them. He at length saw them leave their old homestead and their native city, knowing that for miles and miles in their journey northward they must run the gauntlet of fierce, suspicious faces, and, trembling for the result, he had no rest until he heard of their safety.

One night Dalton's heart was relieved. He had received a letter from the North, written by his little sister Nellie. It ran as follows:

"LOUISVILLE, May 2, 1861.

"DEAR BROTHER DAVY,—

"We reached this smoky, dingy pile of a Louisville yesterday eve. I have half a mind to scold you, dear Davy, for sending us off from our beautiful Savannah. But papa was so glad to get here! One would think, from his manner, that Louisville was next door to heaven. We have had such a dreary journey, it is pleasant to find rest almost any where. Mamma is quite ill from the excitement. Oh, my dear Davy, what does it all mean? What have we been running away from? And why are not you and Harold here? We are all so anxious about you. I am so worried, it seems as if some dreadful thing were going to happen. Won't you and Harold come straight away here to your dear little Nellie? Mamma sends kisses for you both, and papa writes a postscript to this. Every body here is in the greatest excitement, talking about Fort Sumter, and papa says there is going to be a great war. What does it all mean? I have teased papa dreadfully about it, but can get nothing sensible out of him. Do, please, write and tell me every thing, and take the greatest care of Harold.

"From your dear sister,   NELLIE DALTON."

"Papa's postscript" simply, and in few words, described the flight of the family from Georgia across the mountains of East Tennessee, and their safe arrival at Louisville. "Do not be anxious about us," he said. "I have taken enough of my small fortune to keep us in comfort through this season of trouble, which I know will not be over for years yet. We are very anxious about you and Harold. I have no advice to give you, but if you feel compelled to take an active part in this struggle, I know it will be on the side of the dear old Union. And remember, my dear son, if you fight for that, you are at the same time fighting for the South."

Well might little Nellie ask what it all meant, thought Dalton, as, on the evening of the receipt of this letter, he turned the corner of Pulaski Square. He had just left Sarah, the old family servant of the Daltons, with the usual injunction of secrecy as to the movement of the family northward, and with the promise that he would be back before midnight. He was on his way to see Agnes Saumur. Savannah was feverish with excitement. On all sides were to be seen preparations for war. On all sides were to be heard the most confident predictions as to any issue at arms with the cowardly Yankees, and a multitude of curses heaped upon Southern Unionists. What was Agnes thinking of all this time? How would she regard the position which he had resolved to take?

"Oh, here is Mr. Dalton!" was the cry which greeted him as he entered the drawing-room of Agnes Saumur's home.

"We were discussing," said Agnes, "what shall be the true flag of the Southern Republic. Your artistic taste is unquestionable. You shall give us your opinion."

"What is this new flag supposed to represent?" he asked, scarcely venturing at that moment to meet her gaze.

"Why, liberty, of course—the liberty of the South from Lincoln and Yankee abolitionists," said Major Ghilson, who was dressed in uniform. He was captain of a company of the Oglethorpe Guard. At the same time he gazed earnestly, and with a shadow of suspicion crossing his dark face, into the burning eyes of David Dalton, who stood there vainly striving to control the indignant words which rushed to his lips.

"I always thought the stars and stripes were an emblem of liberty. What need have we of another flag?"

"We mean to have nothing about us that savors of the old accursed Union," said Ghilson, advancing toward Dalton. "If I had my way, I would build a wall as high as heaven to separate us from every thing associated with Yankees or the Union. By the way, we have been looking after you, Dalton, this fortnight past. You have had a military education, and will be of service in the war—that is," he added, sneeringly, "if the Yankees will stand before us long enough to be beaten."

"Yes, Mr. Dalton, you must leave the artillery company and join the Oglethorpe Guard," said Agnes, with enthusiasm. He turned and looked into her bright expectant countenance, his anger changing to an expression of sorrow.

B

"Agnes," he said at length, "I can not answer you at this moment."

"Perhaps Dalton has heard that the Oglethorpe Guard has been ordered to join Beauregard's army in Virginia," insinuated Ghilson, in an insolent tone.

Dalton faced him in an instant. "You know, Ghilson, that I am no duelist, or you would scarcely have dared to be so impertinent."

"We will soon meet where you can defend yourself," replied Ghilson, black with passion.

"Perhaps sooner, though not in the place that you imagine," was the calm reply.

Ghilson made no answer, but it was easy to read the revengeful expression of his face, which made Agnes involuntarily shrink from him as he bade her good-night.

Alone with Agnes, Dalton eloquently proclaimed his fealty to the national cause, his hatred of secession, and his intention to depart for the North. "I shall join the Union Army, and, if need be, give my life in defense of the nation."

"Oh, Mr. Dalton, how can you thus desert the South in her extremity. You are a born Southerner. Would you strike at the land of your birth? This is shameful in you," said Agnes, withdrawing the hand which he had taken.

Dalton's face was pale from emotion, but his resolve did not waver, and his voice was firm as he answered her.

"Agnes, this trial is to me a terrible one. I love you above all things—except my country's honor, and that is my honor. Oh, Agnes, you would not have me sacrifice that!"

"I do not know what to say," said Agnes, almost convulsed with her conflicting passions. "I would not have believed that any thing upon earth could have separated us. I thought I could follow you any where. But I never dreamed that you could prove recreant to the South."

"I love the South, and am proud of her glory, and in following my present convictions of right, I renounce no portion of that love and pride. I have no sacrifice to make of past dreams to present emergencies, unless, indeed, you ask me to sacrifice your love, which has been so bright a part of all my dreams, even of my very being, Agnes." As he spoke he drew nearer to her, with a lover's appealing face bent upon hers; and taking from his bosom little Nellie's letter, he said, "I know from this that those who, next to yourself, are the dearest of all to me, are far removed from the insane madness which rules all here. I have remained in this city so long myself but for one purpose, to ask you also to leave and go with me. You have no family ties to bind you to this place. Your parents rest yonder in Bonaventura. Your uncle is hateful to you. I can this very night, by our marriage, give you the protection of my name. Will you not go with me, dear Agnes, away from the turmoil, and suffering, and humiliation which must overtake you in the long years of the bloody, ruinous war before us?" He waited to take her in his arms, but she shrank away from him.

"I will bear all the suffering. Whatever destiny is reserved for the South, I will share," and she looked heroically proud, her heart within her all the while melting with love for David Dalton. "You may be right," she continued, "but to me it seems criminally wrong. I can not follow you. I can not be the wife of a recreant to our cause."

These words stung Dalton's loyal, gentle heart. One moment the two stood gazing into each other's eyes—the next, he was gone, and a giddy, blinding darkness came in his place, as Agnes fell fainting to the floor.

As Dalton passed out of the house, a figure dressed in the gray uniform of the rebel army stepped out from under the shadow of the portico and seized him by the arm.

"Come this way, Dave, and quickly too!"

Dalton's first impulse was to shake off the man's grasp, but he at once recognized the voice as that of his brother.

"Harold! and in that dress! What are you doing here? What's the matter?"

"You'll have to run for it, Dave. Half an hour since Sarah came to our rendezvous. A guard has been stationed at the house to arrest you on your return. She brought over your artillery uniform. Nobody will expect to see you in that, and you must adopt the disguise. Her son Harry has brought his boat around to the marsh, below the saw-mill. You must go down the river. There is no other way of escape. He will take you through the creeks and river over to Charleston. You can get North from there. Something unusual has turned up which excites suspicion."

"I understand it all," said Dalton; "it's Ghilson! But you—what do you propose to do?"

"I will remain. It will throw these devils off the track. Get to the North as fast as you can. I will follow."

In a few moments Dalton had put on his uniform, and, passing fearlessly through the streets, found the boat buried amid the brush of the river-bank, with its dusky pilot waiting in anxious suspense, knowing full well the price of loyalty in these days, and this had not been his first mission in the Union service.

"Good-by, Harold."

"Good-by, Dave."

"Louisville?"

"Louisville."

And with a warm grasp of the hand the brothers parted, not to meet in Louisville in a few weeks, as they anticipated, but long afterward, and under far different circumstances.

III.

WE left Major Dalton, at the close of our first chapter, following the party of captured prisoners whom he found already halted within the inclosure of a light fortification thrown up and used by the enemy during the skirmish of a few hours before.

"I say, Bill," blurted out a tall fellow, with long black hair, whose high cheek-bones and sallow complexion gave him the appearance of an Indian rather than a white man, "it 'pears like as ef we'd seen this place afore."

"D—n me, Jake, ef I didn't work like a nigger throwin' up that ar breastwork." Bill, the speaker, was an unkempt, blear-eyed young soldier, with white, thin lips—a specimen of the "poor white," from his slouching hat to his naked feet, and was one of half a dozen who had been unable to keep up with the rebel column, and had been captured by the Federal cavalry.

"If you have no objection, I would like to ask these men a few questions," said Major Dalton, addressing the officer of the guard.

"Certainly, sir."

"Do any of you belong to a Georgia regiment?" asked Dalton of the group of prisoners.

"No; we came straight from Alabame." "Twenty-third Alabame regiment" two or three responded at the same moment.

"I've bin in Georgy," broke in the man called Jake, "but that was a right smart time back. Come heyar to trade fur niggers, yer see, father 'nd I."

"Thank you," interrupted Dalton; "but I wanted to get news of a brother of mine, Harold Dalton, who I believe was in your service. He came from Savannah."

"I know'd a Mike Dalton afore the war," replied the voluble Jake, "but, ef I remember right, he war shot fur horse-stealing down 'bout New Orleans in fifty-nine."

Dalton was turning away from the inclosure with keen disappointment, when he was recalled by one of the group.

"Major, I think I can give you some information of your brother."

In an instant Dalton was by the side of the speaker, a young man dressed in the uniform of a private, yet whose manner indicated a higher rank.

"I think, sir," he went on to say, "that I helped guard your brother, who was one of a party of deserters on their way to Savannah. If I remember correctly, he had been a conscript, and was caught while attempting to escape to the Yankee lines, just about the time of the Missionary Ridge fight. If he was the man, he was nigh sick to death, and wasn't thought worth the trouble of shooting. At any rate, we turned him over to the guard at Millen."

"Have you heard from him since?" eagerly demanded the major, who for three anxious years had not till this moment received the first token of his brother's fate.

"No, I have not, although I know that some of that party were shot. All of them had been condemned, but, for some special reason which I did not understand, most of them were sent down to Savannah."

"I thank you a thousand times. You have given me a satisfaction I have not known for a long while," said Dalton, as he turned his steps toward his camp-fire at head-quarters. For hours he paced back and forth near his sleeping comrades, heeding not the falling rain. A thousand memories crowded upon his brain. Harold, whom he had last met before his own northward flight, the protracted war not yet closed, a dozen household wrecks of his personal friends, and his own family exiled, but, thank God, secure from harm under the protection of the old flag—these subjects engrossed his thoughts. If there came a memory more insinuating than all others, in which he saw the face of Agnes, sweet, reflective, proud, it was treated like a rude intruder, and was banished with bitter adieus—bitter, but remorseless —repeated, alas! how many times before; for Dalton was a sterner man than he had been—even as the cold, hard face of the North to which he had fled in this time of storms seemed sterner to the view than the warm skies and flowery fields of his native South. To him it was as if the South, with all which it contained beautiful and glorious, and Agnes with the rest, was like a scroll rolled up and sealed until some mighty judgment-day should have passed, when there should arise a new heaven and a new earth. He had not lost hope, but he had now little of that enthusiasm which gives fragrance to hope— which decks her with garlands. He was no doubter, yet Faith was not now the gentle angel she had once been. The very love of Christ was clothed with terrors, as if it were henceforth not to lead men, but only chastise them. Yes, for three years the world had been transformed for Dalton. Like a child that wantons with the very wind that has been blowing its flowers into dust, even so Dalton caught inspiration from the blast of war which had desolated the dreams of his youth. The music ever in his ears was no longer a passionate lyric, but an awful psalm.

IV.

"TO arms! to arms! They come! The wagons! the wagons!" cried Leveridge, in mock heroics, as the first morning light, tinging the western cliffs and lighting up the gloomy gap, revealed to his eyes the white tips of the approaching train and long columns of troops which poured out of the pass, now cleared of obstructions. White signal-flags now took the place of the torches of the night before. The whole encampment was in a moment transformed into a scene of bustling activity. With the wagons had come the entire tribe of head-quarter followers—cooks, servants, orderlies, and what not. Breakfast was on all sides prepared and dispatched with a brevity which would have driven Delmonico's *chef-de-cuisine* out of his wits, and the army was again in motion.

It was that critical moment in the history of Sherman's army when its great leader was looking with intent and eager eyes eastward toward the sea, while with a sidelong, anxious glance he watched most warily the steps of the dashing General Hood. The air was heavy with rumors as various as the straggling speculations out of which they were born. To the merely casual observer the movements ordered and executed at this time seemed to shift this way and that, without definite object, or any well-concerted plan. They were like the fugitive gusts of wind, lifting the dust of the roads and whirling the forest-leaves, preceding the current of the storm which dallies thus by way of prelude, refusing to develop its course or its destination until its strength shall have been matured and its march commenced. Consultations were held by officers high in command, couriers were dispatched hither and thither in opposite directions, but the great movement which these events foreshadowed was only revealed when it began to be accomplished. That movement now belongs to the history of the war, and forms its most interesting chapter.

The morning which looked down upon this bustle of the army found Dalton and Horton apart by themselves. They had climbed to the top of a hill which overlooked the Chattooga River and its picturesque valley. The spectacle offered to their eyes was one characteristic of army life. The river banks were lined with groups of soldiers, some bathing, others washing their clothes, and others lounging on the grass, smoking and chatting in careless ease. From a mill near by emerged a squad of soldiers covered with no small proportion of the flour which they had been grinding from wheat gathered from the country round. Yet farther down the river large details of men were employed sinking in the water huge cribs to answer as piers for a bridge over which the army was to pass. For a time the two gazed upon this scene in silence. They were friends, and there is upon this earth no friendship so full and so enduring as that which binds together the hearts of two strong, earnest soldiers fighting in the same cause. They had received their orders, and knew that they were to part here—Dalton to go to Nashville, and Horton with the main army. They knew that they would not meet again for months—that they might not ever meet again. But there was no expression of sentiment between them; such an expression is not common with men who stand face to face with mighty realities—not that sentiment is a weakness, but because it pales in the presence of instant, pressing action. They looked down into the valley; they saw the movements that were going on, and caught a large measure of their significance in the epic of war in which they were actors; down there was much of tumult and confusion, but their thoughts moved on like the river before them, quick and determined. To them both the immediate future was a promise. To Horton it was the promise of knightly adventure —his was the soul of Sir Launcelot; to Dalton it was like the promised fulfillment of a prophecy. Yet their inmost thought found no vent in words.

At length Dalton, like one waking from a dream, adverted to the topic which, among earthly things, seemed to interest him most of all.

"You will go southward, Horton. In times like these, private interests are of petty consequence, but you know my anxiety in regard to my brother Harold. It is not impossible that you may find some clew to the mystery which has so long perplexed, and which is the occasion of much apprehension to my family. If you do, I know," said he, as he grasped the hand of his friend, "that for my sake, so far as your duties will allow, you will take an interest in his unhappy fate. Last night I learned something from one of our prisoners which gives me hope that he is still alive. You understand me, my friend."

If any other anxious thought occurred to him—if he thought, "You will go seaward, probably—to Savannah, perchance—and should you find one Agnes Saumur, of whom I have *not* spoken to you hitherto, and should you find her in any trouble, you will, for dear love's sake, lighten her care and shield her from want or harm"—if such a thought occurred to his mind, he doubtless said to his heart, "She has chosen to cast her lot with those who are traitors to my country. Let her abide by her choice." At any rate, the name of Agnes Saumur was not spoken.

Horton had scarcely responded with his wonted sympathy to Dalton's request concerning his brother when the two friends were interrupted by an orderly—

"Captain Horton, the general sends for you."

"Is it a long ride?"

"I think so, sir."

"I wish you to go with me; and, if you can find Sam, tell him to put some hard bread into my saddle-bags."

"Yes, captain," and the orderly was gone.

"Good-by, old fellow!" said Horton to his companion, as they neared the line of tents which marked the head-quarters.

"Good-by."

And so they parted—Dalton to join a column of troops moving North, while Horton entered the general's tent.

V.

THE general was seated on a camp-cot. He was a tall, sparely-built man, with a high, reflective head, a nervous, impatient face, which seemed a fit setting for the restless brown eyes that seemed to do duty for all the other organs of sense, observing, comprehending, and deciding at one and the same moment. He was writing with a pencil, earnestly consulting now and then a map which lay before him. Looking up at the sound of footsteps, he exclaimed,

"Horton? Yes, I sent for you. I wish you to go over to General Schofield. He is at Cedar Bluff. Tell him to make that movement across the Coosa at once, and seriously." "I must be certain," he thought to himself, "that Hood has not gone South, after all." "Tell the general that I wish him to report to me his information as frequently and as rapidly as possible. Lose no time, Horton, in getting there and back."

"Yes, general," replied Horton, as he moved away.

"Horton," continued the general, still writing rapidly, "on your way, examine the roads, and report to me their condition."

"Yes, general," and the young aid-de-camp went out from the tent and mounted his horse, which stood waiting for him, in charge of the faithful Baxter.

Threading their way through a column of troops in motion on the road, passing several encampments of troops where the lofty flag-staff marked the headquarters of some division or corps commanders, and then emerging from these streets of canvas houses out into the woods, past a strong detachment posted as the grand guard, over the hills and through the woods again until they reached the outermost pickets, stationed near some ruins which were once some splendid iron-works, Horton received this information—

"It's rayther dangerous, cap'n, to go out on that ar road. The Rebs captured one officer last night nigh on to half a mile out. Yon wood's full on 'em, sir."

If Horton had consulted his own wishes, there is little doubt that he would have turned back for a stronger escort; but his errand was one of haste, and that pride which enters so largely into the motives of a soldier's action impelled him to go on and take the risks. Moreover, his companion was one of the famous First Alabama Cavalry, and not only had the finest instincts of a scout, but knew every foot of the twelve miles to be traversed before reaching the next pickets.

Touching the spur to his horse, the aid-de-camp dashed past the kindly-intending picket, and for a few miles sped swiftly along the road with his companion. In a few moments the young soldier gave little heed to the stony brooks over which he splashed, or to the solemn pines which rose grandly overhead a hundred feet, tufted with spreading green. His thoughts ran, quick as his horse's feet, back to his dear New England. He, too, had his dream of love—a happier dream than any in which his friend Dalton indulged in these days, and one which was every way in harmony with this beautiful morning, and with the spirit of adventure which warmed Horton's soul. Kate Noble stood before him an image of wonderful brilliancy and beauty, her countenance wearing that expression in part so playful and in part so sincere—an expression which could scarcely be called coquettish, but which the French have signified by the term "sensiblerie"—where the poetry of the heart springs up to the surface in countless witcheries of look, and speech, and manner. Born of love, this image was glorified. But Horton dwelt longer and more fondly upon the last moments which he had spent with this charming girl. He recalled every minute detail of that last meeting—his first announcement to her of his purpose to join the Union army, his hesitation to speak of the love which he felt for her, and that final outburst of emotion to which, at parting, she had given full vent—her deeper, finer nature breaking forth in those words, which even yet thrilled every fibre of his being, quickening into life and sustaining the hopes of years—"You will come back to us, dear Alfred! God bless and protect you!" Then her father strode in upon the scene with his crucible, which would turn all things into gold. "My sword shall turn his glittering metal into dross," thought the captain, and almost involuntarily he pressed his spur into his horse's flank, who sprang forward, scattering the twigs and the beds of forest-leaves as if a thunderbolt had fallen among them.

But Horton could not dispel a foreboding of evil as he saw the form of one whom he had befriended in an hour of need lurking among the shadows of his picture, and remembered the words which this Harry Gray had uttered four years ago—"Horton, I believe you are in love with Kate Noble. But I advise you to give up that idea. She does not return such a sentiment, and, even if she did, you have neither the wealth nor the position to satisfy her habitual desires, her tastes, and her ambition." Harry Gray *had* wealth and position. Was he seeking the heart of Kate. Horton had in his pocket letters from home alluding to Gray's assiduous attentions to Miss Noble, and a rumor had reached him that they were engaged to be married—a rumor little heeded by him. "No matter," thought he; "my duty is clear. I am in for the war as long as it lasts, and while God spares my life it shall be cast in the balance against treason."

At this moment his horse shied abruptly, and, glancing to the roadside, Horton saw a rebel—yes, a genuine, undoubted female rebel, with a formidable pair of black eyes, which shot boldly yet beseechingly in his direction. She was plainly dressed in gray homespun, with a light red shawl drawn over her finely moulded shoulders, and which she nervously gathered together with a pair of small and delicate white hands. Her little feet were almost lost in a pair of clumsy "brogs." Her face was really beautiful, though Horton, in his surprise, found no time for photographing it in detail.

"What are you doing out here, with no protector but that negro child? Where is your home?"

"Oh, sir," she said, with sobs and tears, "there are three of your horrible soldiers on our place back here. They tried to force their way into the house, and when we closed the door against them, they threatened to burn it down."

It was not out of his way, and Horton determined to attend to the matter. They soon turned a bend in the road, and arrived at a small, mean dwelling, which looked as if it might be the residence of a plantation overseer. A young girl of about the same age with Horton's newly-found acquaintance stood on the rickety porch. She repeated her sister's complaint, and insisted plaintively, and with some degree of indignation, that Horton should shoot some soldiers who were busily engaged in the adjoining garden digging for sweet potatoes.

Horton concluded, however, to postpone the execution of her wishes for a while, and was watching with some interest his orderly, Baxter, who, leading the horses to and fro, now and then exchanged a few words with a handsome, stalwart negro who had appeared upon the scene. Fearing that he had already diverged too far from his immediate duty, Horton administered a rebuke to the "bummers" in the garden, and was about to take his departure. He prepared to mount, when his movement was arrested by the quick, low tones of the orderly—

"Be careful, captain; there's a rebel officer in that house."

"Ungirth the saddle and take up a hole or two while we are talking. Is he wounded?"

"No; he's a spy, who was inside our lines last night."

"How do you know this?"

"The negro—"

"Yes, I understand."

At once Horton revolved in his mind the entire situation, and decided upon the plan to be pursued. Half a mile up the road he could see the red turbans of the "Zou-zous" disappearing in the woods. An alarm would give the spy an advantage, who, from his concealment, with a pistol, could easily have relieved both captain and orderly from any farther duty in the Union service. No doubt he was watching their movements at this moment, and any act which would indicate on their part any knowledge of his presence might result disastrously to them both, while the spy would escape with important information as to the movements of the Federal troops on the previous day.

What was to be done? In an attempt at capture, and the fight which would follow, the chances were about equal, for the two women were of that daring and romantic nature which would prompt them to look upon such an adventure as a favorable opportunity for a remarkable display of female heroism. But the spy *must* be captured, and there was no time for delay. As Baxter was tightening the girth, Horton whispered to him,

"Take both horses to the end of the house, on the right. The rebel must be in that room. Hitch the horses, if you can. Be on the watch if he attempts an escape, and, in any event, act at discretion." He could trust Baxter, whom he had seen before in more critical situations than the present.

Horton walked up to the house, while Baxter led the horses toward the appointed destination.

"I am sorry to trouble you, ladies," he said, carelessly, "until my orderly repairs a slight damage in my saddle;" and then, heedless of their affrighted faces, he rushed past them, entered the house, bolted the door behind him, and, advancing with a quick step, he placed his heavy cavalry boot against the door of the room in which he suspected that the spy was hid. It gave way, and he landed, amid a cloud of dust, in the centre of the room. It was very much as he had apprehended. The spy was at that moment thrusting a handful of papers into the fireplace, and was holding in one hand a lighted match for their destruction. But he was one moment too late. Turning suddenly at the sound of Horton's footstep, he raised his pistol and fired, fortunately for Horton, in great haste and harmlessly. The next moment Horton's sword-point was at his breast.

"Surrender," shouted Horton, "or you're a dead man!"

"Never!" cried the Confederate, with an oath.

Just then the assailant's sword-arm was arrested from behind; a pair of white arms hung about his neck, and for the instant he was disarmed.

"Run, Albert, run for your life!" screamed the black-eyed friend of the spy.

But Albert seemed indisposed to leave his antagonist in that interesting situation. He cocked his pistol for another shot, but seemed unwilling to risk the chance of injuring the girl, who still hung heavily upon Horton's neck. Muttering a fierce curse, he strode toward the door, turning for a single glance toward his enemy. This was a slight tactical error, for Baxter, hearing the pistol-shot, had entered the rear door, and had arrived upon the scene at the most interesting point in the proceedings. With what is technically known as a "front cut," he struck at the spy's head. Unfortunately, his sabre's point, in making the circle, came in contact with the low ceiling of the cabin, and the weapon fell harmlessly at his side. The spy hurled Baxter against the wall, and dashed from the room. But he now met with an unexpected opponent. Filling up the outer doorway stood the negro, whom he tried in vain to turn aside. There followed a brief, terrible struggle, and the spy's knees struck under, and he fell.

"You have killed him!" cried Horton, as he ran forward and knelt by the side of the prostrate body, and felt the inanimate pulse of the hand, which still, in its rigid grip, held a glittering knife.

"It was my life or his, sir. I know the man," replied the negro, as he thrust his bowie-knife into his belt. "It's Nelson, one of the most desperate scouts in the Confederate service."

"Do you belong to this place?"

"No, sir; I came here with this man."

"And yet you killed him. There is something here which I do not quite comprehend. But we have no time for explanation. You must come along with me. I will send a guard," he said to the frightened women, "and have this fellow buried."

Gathering the papers scattered upon the hearth

and all others which he could find upon the lifeless body, Baxter got the horses in readiness, and, with Horton and the negro, who had found a mule in the stable, they proceeded on their military errand.

VI.

AS soon as the party got well out upon the road, Horton called to his orderly—

"Baxter, I shall ride on to the Bluffs. You will remain behind, and come more slowly with this man."

"Yes, captain."

And Horton was off again through the woods with headlong speed, nor did he slacken his pace till he reached the picket-guard.

"Dispatches for General Schofield" was his answer to the challenge, and the young officer pressed on again until, at length, with throbbing flank and distended nostril, and reeking with foam, his noble mare halted at Schofield's head-quarters. The message was delivered, and, while the answer was preparing, the papers of the Confederate spy were examined, and proved to be of great value. Meanwhile Baxter had reported, the negro was brought in, and, in answer to the questions put him, revealed additional matters of importance. In a few moments Horton was once more in the saddle. The negro accompanied the captain and his orderly on the return. He was a well-formed, strong man, full six feet in height, and had a remarkable face. At the first glance little trace of negro blood could have been observed in him. His hair was long and almost straight, his face was nearly white, oval in form, with black eyes, and an aquiline nose, with no more expansion of nostril than is often found in one of pure Caucasian blood. His lips were thin, his jaw square, his chin round and finely formed. The face seemed gentle; yet, as the captain recalled the events of the morning, he remembered an almost demoniacal expression in the man's face during the conflict with the spy, no trace of which was now discoverable. He wore now an expression of lassitude and dejection, which was evidently of a mental rather than a physical character.

"Why did you betray your master this morning?"

A slight flush mounted to the man's forehead at this abrupt interrogation, but he looked firmly into the eyes of his questioner.

"He was not my master. I gave him up because he had information of value to these rebels."

"What is your name?"

"Zimri, sir."

"That is an odd name. Zimri, you have a last name?"

"I am a slave, sir. I need not tell you, therefore, that I have never known any name but Zimri."

"How came you with that spy?"

"I was sent by my master—my half-brother, General Ralph Buford, commanding a brigade of Wheeler's cavalry."

"Does your brother trust you so implicitly as to permit you to come into our lines?"

"Sometimes I think he wishes I would never come back."

"Why?" asked Horton, somewhat mystified.

"My mother," replied Zimri, "was a quadroon, and the slave of our father. We were nursed from the same bosom, and grew to manhood on the same plantation—I the slave, and he my brother and master. A few years ago, my brother married the daughter of one of the wealthy planters of South Carolina. When she came to our home she brought with her a quadroon girl, who was really her mistress's companion, though nominally a slave. Charlotte and I loved each other, and were married before the war." Zimri stopped there. He seemed overcome with strong emotion. His face wore something of the expression of the morning, only more intense and violent. If there was something more—the natural continuation of the narrative—it was evidently something which Zimri could not trust himself to speak. He seemed absorbed in some bitter recollection—some vision of the past which troubled and angered him. He recalled the too vivid picture of his master's first vision of Charlotte, his expression of undisguised admiration of her beauty, and the ill-disguised devil of lust which lurked behind his admiration; he traced through its stages of increasing darkness the cloud which from that moment settled upon his life, but he could not express his thoughts in words. At length he resumed his story:

"In the third year of the war, Buford's regiment was ordered to Virginia, and for ten months Charlotte and I enjoyed the great happiness of our home. Then came the day when Bragg was pressing the starved army of Rosecrans at Chattanooga, and Longstreet's corps was transferred to the battle-field of Chickamauga. Then followed the campaign which resulted in Sherman's capture of Atlanta. It was after this conflict, and while the two armies were taking breath, that Buford, promoted to a brigadier general, visited his home, and, on his departure for the field again, he ordered my wife and myself to go with him. I entreated that Charlotte might be left behind. But the general was inexorable, and, of course, he had no explanation to make to his slaves!"

"The fact is," he said, "you've had a lazy time of it on the plantation. You are not needed here. You can't raise any cotton. The d—d Yankees have shut up all the ports, and we can only cultivate breadstuffs. Overseer Sam can attend to the corn crop and get it in; to-morrow we start for the army."

"Perhaps," continued Zimri, "you can understand why he intrusts me upon the most perilous expeditions, and would rather that I should never return."

Horton knew too much of the operation of the slave system on the plantation to wonder much at the revelation thus made, but he was moved none the less with sympathy for Zimri.

"And what do you propose to do now?" he asked.

"I must return to the rebel lines, with your permission. I know that there is work for me to do there;" and the expression of his face indicated that it was no ordinary work—a work of vengeance upon the tyrants of his race.

"I think there will be no difficulty in your going back, so far as we are concerned; I will consult with others about that; but can you traverse the country and enter the enemy's lines in safety?"

"There is no fear upon that point. I have a pass which will protect me from rebel troops, and as to marauders, this knife," pointing to the bowie in his waist-belt, "is as useful as your revolver."

By this time the party had approached the spot where the pickets of the Union army were stationed in the morning, and where Horton had been warned of horrible danger. To the surprise of the latter, in the place of the shelter-tents and the parked wagons there was a vacant waste. A few patches of cotton, which had served as a soldier's couch, here and there whitened the ground; the remains of the carcasses of beeves attracted several hungry-looking curs; a few camp-fires were still smouldering on the field, but the army had gone.

Horton, after a moment's thought, drew from his pocket a card, and wrote,

"The bearer is my servant Zimri. Guards and pickets will pass him through our lines.

"ALFRED HORTON, Capt. U. S. A. and A. D. C."

Giving this to Zimri, he said,

"I am reposing a trust in you which, of course, I believe is deserved. I shall not venture to advise you as to your present sad situation, but whenever you wish, come to this army, and, if I am alive, you will find in me a friend."

"Thank you, sir. You may see me again some time."

Thus Horton parted with Zimri. Baxter in the mean while had learned from a straggler the direction of the army. As Horton turned off from the road to cross the bridge which spanned the Chattooga, he could see Zimri on the western hill-top, his erect form cut sharp and clear against the rich twilight sky, and then it suddenly disappeared behind a projecting rock. It was far into the night when the captain and his companion reached the camp, and there he heard that the final order had been issued for the great March to the Sea.

VII.

SWEDENBORG says, in his "True Christian Religion," "The Africans excel all other Gentiles in clearness of interior judgment." Whether or not the great Swedish seer ever penetrated the mysteries of the spiritual world, or whether this view of the African race is to be accepted as an inspired truth, certain it is, both from the universal testimony of their masters and from all the experiences of the war, that the mind of the negro race, as it has exhibited itself in the South of America, is receptive, sympathetic, and affectionate in the highest degree. Their acquiescence in a condition of absolute servitude is not by any means to be attributed, as it so often is, to an inherent and hereditary meanness of spirit, but partly to their trust that God would set them free in His own good time, and to their gentle and impressionable nature. Though in the early days of the war it was confidently predicted that the negroes would rise in insurrection upon the first opportunity, there is no evidence of any attempt on their part to throw off their yoke by rising against their masters, even after the Emancipation Proclamation was issued, the knowledge of which, in a few days, had spread over every plantation in the South. The truth is, there was a philosophy, or what Swedenborg calls a clearness of interior judgment, in the negro character, which was never understood by the masters, on account of the servile circumstances which partially stifled and wholly disguised its development.

Because the negro was led by the Christian faith, which took deep root in his gentle, yielding heart, to display unexampled forbearance, it must not therefore be supposed that he was destitute of the stronger elements of human nature. These also were perverted and disguised by their servitude. As the affection of a slave is lowly, and seems therefore of a baser sort, so his pride, from the very necessity of concealment, creeps rather than climbs, and not unfrequently assumes the mask of revenge, simply because, being pressed down to the earth, and driven into dark ways, it naturally uses base means for the accomplishment of its ends.

Zimri was an exceptional character under the slave

system. Although less than three fourths white, he gave few external indications of African descent. Usually his nature was gentle, almost as a woman's, but from his father he had inherited—unhappily for one doomed to slavery—a proud determination, which, under other circumstances, might have won him success and fame in almost any sphere of life, but which, in slavery, proved a curse.

When Zimri left Captain Horton, he traveled westward, directly across the hills and through the woods, avoiding the main roads and even the forest paths, for he had no desire to come into contact with detachments or foraging parties of either army. He journeyed thus for hours steadily on, until he came upon a road which, from the distance he had traversed, he felt sure must be the route leading north from Gadsden, where, three days before, he had left Hood's army. Dismounting from his mule, he examined by the moonlight the wagon tracks which here and there had cut deep into the yielding earth. The footmarks all pointed northward, but Zimri had doubts to which army they belonged. Leading his patient mule by the bridle, he walked along the road for several rods, when he came upon the carcass of a mule who, worn out with a too exhausting pilgrimage, had sunk down and died by the roadside. Lifting one of its feet, Zimri counted the nails in its shoes. "One, two, three on a side. The Yankees are more generous with their heel-taps. The rebels must have passed here, and not long since either, for the body of the poor beast is scarcely cold."

The sun had risen above the mountain-tops behind him ere Zimri came upon the pickets guarding the rear of Hood's army.

"Oh, it's only that cursed white nigger of the general's," remarked a sentinel to a companion.

"You've come to the right place, nig. Yer master's in that ar cabin yonder across the creek."

"Yes, I see the house. Have there been any Yankees round here?"

"Nary a Yank. The blue-bellies keep clar of the Rattlesnake Brigade. Cuss 'em, they don't like the smell of powder—hey, Smithers?" The last part of this remark was addressed to a comrade, for Zimri had pushed on toward the house, which could be seen in the middle of a patch of cleared ground a few hundred yards up the road. As he approached the place he noticed an unusual bustle, betokening a hasty movement forward. A trumpeter stood near the corner of the house, ringing out from his bugle, in shrill notes, the call, "To boot and saddle." On the roadside, and in the meadow bordering upon the creek, hundreds of men were gathering in haste, preparing to mount. Negroes were rushing about the yard, and in and out of the cabin, packing mess-chests in the wagons, with other camp equipage. In front of the house, booted and spurred, stood a tall man of dark complexion, whose dress of gray cloth bore the insignia of a general of cavalry. Long and thin black hair fell in profusion over his shoulders. In his hands, small as a woman's, he held a paper, which he was reading attentively. The most peculiar feature of this altogether striking physiognomy was the nose. It did not seem to belong of right to the face, which had a haughty and despotic expression. It was broad and flat, as if it had been borrowed from the blackest negro about the camp. This was General Ralph Buford. And he had come by his nose legitimately, for his grandmother had been one of a class who are by courtesy designated as "Creole." By that inexplicable freak of nature which causes a physical or mental characteristic to leap over one generation and then reappear, the African blood of his ancestors boldly proclaimed itself in General Buford's most prominent feature. Looking at the two brothers, a stranger would have found it difficult to determine which was the master and which the slave.

As Zimri passed up a side-path leading to the rear of the house, he gave little heed to the presence of the general, for his quick eye had caught sight of a fluttering handkerchief waved by Charlotte in token of recognition. He had scarcely dismounted before his wife, running from the shelter of a tent, had caught him in her arms, exclaiming, in broken words of love and gladness,

"Oh, Zimri! thank God you's come back. I was afraid you might be killed or wounded. You's come back now. Oh, don't go away again!"

Zimri made no answer, but pressed her in silence, and almost convulsively, to his heart, and then, holding her away, looked into her face with his tender, searching eyes. In truth it was a lovely picture, as she stood there with the rich blood mantling her neck and face to the temples, and as the flush died away, leaving a golden light upon her countenance, as if the sunlight had just passed over and kissed it. Her dress of coarse homespun showed marks of camp life, but its dinginess could not disguise her beauty, nor conceal the contour of her graceful form; while her eyes, which were neither black nor brown, but black and brown—a golden color—modestly drooping, shone out with a clear pure light, which banished from her husband's mind all doubt and misgiving. His voice trembled as he said,

"Charlotte, if I had my own way, we should never be parted from each other. Only twice have I met and caressed you thus since we left the plantation, but you know it is no fault of mine."

Charlotte was really glad to see her husband, and would gladly have fled with him any where, even into the lines of the Union army. But their meeting was soon interrupted by a higher power, which claimed submission from them both.

"General, I see your man Zimri has come back," said Major Ghilson, who stood near Buford, giving orders to those about him.

"Zimri!" shouted the general, his eyes angrily resting upon the couple, whom he had for the first time discovered, "come here!"

Zimri did not answer immediately, but, drawing Charlotte closer to him, kissed her most tenderly and affectionately.

"We will escape, if it is possible," he said, and then advanced to where his brother stood, whose thin lips and distended nostrils gave evidence of uncontrollable passion and rage.

"When did you come back from the scout?"

"Five minutes ago."

"Is Nelson here?"

"No, sir."

"Where did you leave him?"

"Back near the Coosa. We were attacked, became separated, and I escaped."

"Yes, *you* manage always to return with a whole skin. Which way were the d—d Yankees moving?"

"It was impossible to ascertain."

Buford was disappointed, and in the worst of humors. But he had just received explicit orders from Hood indicating that a column of the enemy was moving toward Chattanooga, and that there was a rumor that a still larger column was somewhere in the vicinity of Rome, and commanding him to report to Wheeler at once, who had been instructed to keep in front of this latter column in the event of its moving southward. He had no time, therefore, to waste upon Zimri.

"Ghilson, I want you to move your regiment south of the Coosa. I shall follow quickly."

"Zimri, you will go with Ghilson. Charlotte will follow with my head-quarters."

Zimri made no answer, but there was that in his face which his master did not take the trouble to interpret, but which surely boded the latter no good, and was in striking contrast with the slave's submissive silence.

And so Zimri rode off with Ghilson, unable to speak one word of hope or encouragement to Charlotte. Many weary weeks and months of suffering passed before he saw her again, and then—

VIII.

NAPOLEON'S maxim, that "an army may pass wherever a man can plant his foot," is of easier application to the mountainous district of which he was speaking than to the swamps and marshes before Savannah, where Sherman's army settled down after the bold march from Atlanta.

These morasses stretch away on a dead level for many miles from the sea-coast. Here and there by some river's side, a bluff, formed perhaps ages ago by the action of the sea, raises its head above the monotonous level, but with these rare exceptions the country was low, and covered with the decayed vegetation of centuries. The sun of this tropical climate, and an unfailing supply of water, have caused the growth of the most luxuriant foliage. Vast forests of pine, groves of live-oak and water-oak, clusters of the beautiful magnolia, of the gloomy cypress, and of the ugly and unfruitful palmetto, with a thousand varieties of weed matted together into an almost impenetrable undergrowth, encompassed the army in its march through this region. In the summer season, this luxuriant combination of curious and ever-varying shapes with the most magical colors must appear like a miracle of beauty. But in the December of 1864, when the Northern army traversed these illimitable marshes, the spectacle was unattractive. For many miles the roads—or, rather, the raised causeways—led through these gloomy shades in undeviating straight lines. The weary soldier found it impossible to turn aside to right or left, for on either side of him lay the treacherous swamp. Here and there, at wide intervals, upon some oasis in the dreary desert, a few negro cabins marked the site of a rice or a cotton plantation, affording relief both to the eye and to the weary feet of the wanderers. Off to the right, upon the banks of the Ogeechee, were open rice-fields, through which ran numerous canals used for flooding the rice at certain stages of its growth. Raised causeways, carefully constructed, traversed these plantations, leading from the negro quarters to the various mills situated on the banks of the small streams.

It is true that up to this point the army had enjoyed an uninterrupted succession of holidays, living upon turkeys, chickens, and "soft-tack," as the soldiers term the bread which they make for themselves. But the transportation was limited, and the abundant supply of food in the earlier stages of the march could not be made available for any future needs; and although Sherman had foreseen the possibility of such an emergency as now arose, and had given repeated instructions to the subordinate commanders always to keep the supply-trains full, and to issue rations from them only when it was absolutely necessary, yet, when the necessity came, these supplies were soon exhausted. The sixty thousand soldiers, twenty thousand black refugees, and the horses, mules, and cattle, quickly emptied the wagons. Actual suffering there was none, because there was plenty of rice and a large number of beeves; yet rice and beef formed a diet whose long continuance would soon have decimated the ranks. The change from abundance to scarcity was marked, and produced much illness and demoralization. But, under all difficulties, the army was saved from perilous discontent by the sublime faith which it had in its great leader.

Colonel Barnard's brigade formed a part of the extreme left of the line toward the Ogeechee. The plantation on which his camp was located afforded little in the way of forage; the reserved rations had been consumed, and both the men and the cattle were compelled to resort to the rice and rice-straw left on the place in large quantities. . .

The colonel, with several of his officers, one evening sat watching a group of soldiers and negroes who were pounding the rice in big mortars made from the trunks of trees.

"These mortars come into good play just now, since our soldiers can not have patent labor-saving machines to carry with them," said Oakland. "See that soldier there, he's making the most out of the situation."

The soldier referred to had cut a bit of pork from a hog slaughtered not ten minutes before. This he was now frying in a tin plate, dexterously balanced between two logs, over a bed of live coals. Into the pan he poured the bruised rice, which had been mixed into a sort of paste. The batter was soon nicely browned and removed, making way for a slice of fresh beef. This cooked, a kettle of boiling coffee was lifted from the fire, and a plain but delectable meal was set before the small group of soldiers.

The notice of the officers was soon diverted from this and other similar scenes of the hour by the sound of heavy artillery and musketry firing in the direction of the front, filling the woods with a thousand sharp and resonant echoes.

"We must see what this means," said Barnard, turning toward Oakland; but his young adjutant had already started up the pathway cut through the bushes, and leading to the trenches.

"I'll go with you, colonel," said Leveridge, as he threw into the fire the blazing brand from which he had lighted his pipe.

As the two officers strode away into the timber, the firing, which had lulled for an instant, burst forth afresh. Screaming shells whirled and smashed through the branches of the trees overhead, while the z-z-z-ip of some overshot bullet sped pleasantly and harmlessly along among the leaves and twigs. Very soon they encountered wounded men limping along, and then the stretchers with their freight of men hurt to the death.

"Are you badly hurt, Morton?" asked Barnard of a solitary soldier leaning against a tree for partial support, the red blood streaming down his face from a wound in the forehead.

"No, colonel, thank you. It's only a flesh-wound; but the bandage came off."

"What's the row out there?"

"Our picket line saw an opening, and made for

the enemy's rifle-pits, and, by George! we got 'em. They're trying to take 'em back, but they'll have a tough job of it."

The two officers were approaching a dangerous quarter, and were obliged to creep along for a little distance to a line of earth-works, behind which lay a long line of soldiers, who were taking an active part in the engagement.

"What's the situation, major?" asked Barnard of an officer busily engaged in giving orders to the command.

"Well, you see," replied the officer, "the Rebs have been trying to drive back our picket line, to prevent our shutting up that sixty-four pounder which bothered us so much yesterday. The boys are a little mad, and have been giving them 'Hail Columbia,' driving them back thus far, and I think we can hold our own, though it's an important position for them to recover. We've got the dead wood on 'em, sir, if you can get up the right of the line. Our left rests on a swamp as rotten as the cursed Confederacy."

"You've done a splendid thing, major; but we must cover the right, or they'll find our weak spot, and double on us."

"No fear for to-night, colonel. They've made two

assaults, and about as many have taken up ground in eternity as went back."

The prostrate figures in gray and brown uniforms in the stubble-field just ahead corroborated the statement of the major.

"Barnard," said Leveridge, "I am going back, and will report the situation to the general, and you shall have all the support you want in less than half an hour."

"Oakland," said Barnard, "you'd better go with Leveridge."

As Oakland moved away from under the hottest fire, he saw one Kelly, a private of his regiment, who had established a reputation for cowardice which was unworthy his Irish blood. He was accompanying to the rear a soldier who had received a flesh-wound in the arm.

"Where are you going, Kelly?" he asked. "You are wanted here. Don't you see the rebels coming again?"

"Yis, I say the murthering blackguards," answered the frightened Irishman, ducking his head to a twelve-pound round-shot. "Shure an' don't I both say and hear? but—oh, Holy Mother, protect me!—you wouldn't have me leave a wounded comrade to die upon the faild of battle, would you?"

"Kelly, you are a disgrace to the regiment. You are not seriously wounded?" turning to the comrade whom Kelly had taken in charge.

"No, sir," was the reply. "I did not see Kelly until I had reached the timber. It's all humbug about his helping me, colonel."

"I thought so. As you pass head-quarters, give him over to the guard."

The assistance which Leveridge had promised was soon sent to Barnard, who, with this support, was able to keep his new vantage-ground.

Upon his return to camp, Oakland made it one of his first duties to look after the recreant Kelly. This fellow had been severely punished upon several occasions for cowardice and drunkenness. He possessed few of the virtues of his countrymen, and many of their vices. Remarkably reticent and shy during an engagement, after the danger was all over he gave full play to his tongue and to his imagination, describing feats of valor performed by himself which were more remarkable than the deeds of Sancho Panza.

On this particular night, Kelly and a brother Milesian had obtained some apple-jack, and found themselves joyously drunk in a guard-tent.

Oakland had snatched a few hours' sleep, and was

walking back and forth with anxious thought. The shouts of the victory of the afternoon could not hush the night-wind, which brought to his ears the moans of wounded and dying men, broken in upon continually by the firing of the faithful pickets, or the smothered distant boom of cannon.

He had several times checked the boisterous noise of the drunken Irishmen. By-and-by their talk was carried on in a lower tone—

"I say," whispered Kelly, "O'Brien, are you aslape at such a time? Don't you hear the roar of the inemy's cannon?"

"Oh, bother the inemy's cannon. Don't I know that I'm in the guard-house for getthing thrunk?"

"An' you're right there, my boy. It all comes o' them officers. An' sure, ar'n't they stuck up all the while—a puttin' on airs as if they owned the whorld? Faith, O'Brien, the soldiers and officers nowadays are not so patriotic and self-sacrificing as the heroes of the Revolution were. Didn't they give up the last cint, and suffer? Arrah, there was no six-hoss mule transportation-wagons in them days. Shure, O'Brien, and didn't George Washington, the fayther, sir, of his counthry, walk inter the city of Boston with his valeese in his hand?"

"You say that Gineral Washington walked inter

the strates of Boston with a valeese in his hand? Now, how do you know that, Kelly? Shure an' you wasn't there."

This rather bothered Kelly for a moment, but he rallied and said,

"Noa, but me forefaythers wos, thank God."

Soon, by the capture of Fort McAllister, the sole hinderance to the outlet seaward had been overcome. Just after this event, a party of officers, several participants, and others, witnesses of the grand achievement, were threading their way among the dead and wounded, who lay as they fell near the fort. They were escorted by an orderly through the mesh of limbs of trees which had been thrown together for an abatis, and through the thickly-planted torpedoes, and were then guided to a light foot-bridge which spanned the wide ditch, and led to the sally-port cut in the parapet.

"There is a row-boat moored in the river near the fort?" said the commanding general of the army, who spoke as if he knew that a boat ought to be there.

"Yes, general."

"Select four good men to man the boat. I must go down the river," he continued, addressing one of his principal subordinate officers, "and find the steamer which we signaled this afternoon. Our communication with the fleet must be established at once."

It was a hazardous undertaking for the general to face the peril of guerrillas along the banks, and the still more dangerous torpedoes in the river. He was not familiar with the windings of the stream even in the daytime. For all that, he certainly knew the boat might as easily lose its way, and ascend some bay or estuary into the enemy's lines, as go directly to the little steamer, which lay, an undistinguishable spot, upon the water many miles toward Ossibaw Sound. "But," said he, as some of his staff alluded to the perils of the expedition, "over there in those swamps are sixty thousand of my men, who are hungry to-night. I must see for myself what means are provided for giving them food. Besides, danger is the rule and not the exception in our soldier-life, you know."

Hardly had the words been spoken when a loud explosion was heard immediately behind the group. All turned quickly at the sound, and saw a stream of flame shoot up from the earth into the darkness, and by its lurid light could be distinguished the agonized face and mangled form of a soldier who had trod upon one of the buried torpedoes. It was a significant response to the sentiment just expressed by the general, and no one ventured to break the silence, but all watched with bated breath the preparations for launching the boat. In a few moments all was ready, and the general descended the bank and entered the boat, accompanied only by the distinguished commander of his right wing. That officer, always calm, brave, and just, called out to the group upon the shore, and said, "Gentlemen, if we should not return, you will remember that General Slocum is in command of this army. Good-night!" and the boat, with its precious freight, shot off into the darkness.

Horton wandered away from the party of officers to the parapet of the fort, on one of the sides which had been assaulted that day. Bomb-proofs and traverses loomed up against a sky partially illumined by the moonlight. At his feet, dark, placid, and treacherous, ran the Ogeechee. Within the fort, around flickering fires, leaning against ponderous cannon, were groups of soldiers, talking over the exciting incidents of the day. Stretched upon the ground all around him lay dead and dying men. Just at his feet, dressed in Union blue, lay a sergeant of the line. His white face wore a sweet and gentle expression, and, but for the fixed stare of the eyes, one would have thought him sleeping. He lay just as he had fallen when he received that ragged wound near the heart.

It was a weird and solemn spectacle, and, as Horton gazed around and down into the face of the dead, an indescribable awe crept over him. Finally, as if seeking a contrast to such terrible scenes, his thoughts reverted to the dear old home. Again he lived over the parting scene with Kate in the library; again the words of the blue-eyed, flaxen-haired girl sounded in his ears, "You will come back to me. God bless you!"—and again, also, more vividly than ever before, he saw another face intruding itself upon the picture. It was a selfish face, and, as Horton recalled it, the man to whom it belonged seemed to be telling some story of meanness or dishonor, for his lips wore a cold, cynical sneer, while his eyes gleamed with a wicked stare, as if he were glad to pierce and crush the fresh-blooming flower before him, while she, defiant, yet in tears, repelled the accusation.

About midnight the general returned up the river. He had succeeded in communicating with the fleet. In three days from that time, Captain Boutelle, of the Coast Survey, had removed a score of torpedoes from the river, and steam-boats, heavily laden with army supplies of every description, came safely up the tortuous channel to King's Bridge, where suitable preparations had been made for the reception and distribution of their welcome freight.

D 2

IX.

AT this moment, when Savannah was almost, but not quite in the possession of the Union army, let us enter the streets of the beleaguered city, and, shutting our ears to the rumors of every sort that are flying as fast and as tumultuously as the Confederate cavalry, this way and that, over the city, let us follow the footsteps of Agnes Saumur as she moves along Bull Street, then down Brighton, and across the market square out toward the stockade, near the railroad dépôt. She was dressed in black, and closely veiled.

"You can't see any of the pris'ners to-day, ma'am," was the response of the sentinel, as she was about to enter the gate.

"You do not recógnize me. I have been in the habit of coming here for two years past."

"I know'd you well 'nuff, but thar's a new officer in command. He says thar's too much of this stuffin' the cursed Yanks. He's put a stop to it."

"Where is the officer? May I not be permitted to speak to him?"

"Oh, he'll see you. He likes ter look at pretty wimmen. We found that out soon 'nuff. That's his office, near that gun, ter the right."

Agnes gathered her veil still closer about her face, and, having been admitted to the officer's quarters, and glanced at the face of its military occupant, she would have retreated, but it was too late.

"Can I be of service to you, madam?"

"Yes, sir; I wish to visit a prisoner under your charge."

"That, I regret to say, madam, is against the rules," said the officer, while he sought to penetrate the thick crape veil which concealed the face of the applicant; "but I may make an exception in your case. Whom do you wish to see?"

Agnes hesitated a brief instant, and then replied,

"Harold Dalton."

"Harold Dalton," repeated the officer, and then, turning to an adjutant who was sitting at a desk, he inquired,

"Is that Dalton a brother of the Dalton who is in the Yankee army?"

"Yes, sir," replied the adjutant. "They used to live in this city before the war. This Dalton was condemned to be shot a year ago, but was reprieved, and has been in hospital ever since."

"Is David Dalton in the Federal army?" asked Agnes, stepping forward. "Where? in what army?"

"Yes, miss, David Dalton is in the Yankee army," replied the officer. "Why are you interested in his whereabouts? Excuse me, but when a person comes to visit a criminal whose brother is a traitor to the South, I have a right to ask questions."

"I wish to inform this sick brother, who for four years has not heard a word from his family."

As Agnes concluded her last remark, which came tremblingly from her lips, an expression of recognition passed across the officer's dark face.

"Captain," he said to the adjutant, "I shall not need you for a while."

As soon as the door closed, he lifted a crutch from the table, and, leaning upon it, advanced toward Agnes.

"If I am not mistaken, I am speaking to Agnes Saumur?"

She withdrew her veil, and answered with calmness,

"You are right, Major Ghilson, but I would much rather have avoided this recognition. I thought you were in the field."

"I was in the field, Agnes," he said, with some bitterness, "until a fortnight since, and, if it had not been for a cursed Yankee bullet, you might have been spared the pain of seeing me here. But, so far was I from understanding that such a meeting would give you pain, I have tried to find you out, that I might renew a pleasant acquaintance. But I was baffled in my search. Town friends seem to have been deserted by you—at least they could give me no information. But I seem to have made a great mistake. You appear to have more sympathy with these Yankees than with your former friends."

"Since my uncle's death I have been secluded. I do not desire to go into society. Besides, it is undoubtedly true that my opinions in regard to the events of the last four years have undergone a decided change."

"Well, I do not wish to discuss with you about these matters, Agnes. Do you remember that, three years ago, you encouraged me in the belief that you would one day be my wife? To all my letters to you you have vouchsafed but one reply, and that came two summers ago. I was in the mountains of Tennessee. The words were, 'You have presumed too much upon my friendship. I did not love you. I can not be you wife.'"

Ghilson's face expressed bitter disappointment and burned with vehement passion as he tore from a packet drawn from his pocket a letter—the one to which he had just alluded—and held it before this woman, who shrank from the paper with an expression of agony.

"God help me," she moaned, "but I never anticipated this. I loved, but, Major Ghilson, I did not love you. I—"

Ghilson interrupted her with an oath, while the letter held in his nervous fingers fell crumpled at her feet.

"I believe you all the time loved that scoundrel Dalton!" he exclaimed.

This outburst roused Agnes from her grief. She no longer thought of the unhappy past. "What right," she asked, "had this man to call David Dalton a scoundrel?"

"He may differ with you as to what constitutes patriotism, but you know him to be a loyal-hearted man. He is incapable of a mean word or act. He is no scoundrel, Major Ghilson. But let us not talk of these things longer. It can only embitter my life, which, Heaven knows, has seen enough of sorrow. I beg of you, sir, to permit me to visit Harold Dalton. He is just recovering from a long illness, and needs such nursing as the attendants here are unable to give him."

"Agnes Saumur, it is an easy thing for you to ask me to forget the past. Do you think I can also forgive? No; the words of that cruel letter are burned into my soul. No; this Harold Dalton may parch with thirst, but *you* shall not give him a drop of water. He may die of want—of the hunger of body and soul, but you shall not minister to him. Hear me—"

But Agnes, chilled with horror at Ghilson's fearful rage, would not listen longer, but hastened from the room, across the yard, and out of the gate. Her first thought was simply to fly from Ghilson's presence, the second was to obtain succor for her friend Dalton. Impelled by this latter thought, she sought General Hardee's head-quarters. But the general could not be seen that day; he would be at leisure on the morrow. But she did not know that the morrow would witness the evacuation of the city by the Confederates, and the triumphant entry of Sherman's army.

X.

EITHER General Hardee received information of some new movement of the besieging army which would have closed the only avenue of escape left him, or else his military judgment divined that a flanking operation was the next thing in order. Certainly, whatever influenced him, on the morning of the 21st of December he had decamped from the city, and the Federal army was soon in possession of the magnificent prize—"a Christmas present to the nation," as Sherman called it. For two days the national troops poured through the streets of the city. For two long, weary days Agnes Saumur sat at her window watching, with tearful eyes, the throng of soldiers, and the flags that seemed to wave gentle recognition to her; but the one presence after which her heart yearned now with the fondest longings was not there, and there was occasion enough for despair in this to spoil for her what otherwise would have been the most joyous drama of her life.

"What right have I to love him?" she asked herself, and she stared hopelessly out upon the long train of wagons that followed the column of troops.

"I tinks Massa Dalton's not in that 'ar comp'ny, Miss Agnes," ejaculated the old negress Sarah, who had been for some time sitting behind her mistress.

Sarah had remained in Agnes's service after the Daltons had left Savannah. During the long four years no word had passed between them concerning David Dalton, yet underneath her rough, scarred skin there beat a big, sympathizing heart. In the keenness of her perceptions, which had been sharpened by years of secret observation, and with that womanly instinct which divines more than it sees, she had penetrated the inmost heart of Agnes Saumur.

But Agnes did not turn her face from the window.

"Who spoke of Mr. Dalton, Sarah?"

"Dar's nobody dat I knows on; but I heerd dat he's in the Yankee army. God bress me, missus, see de beautiful flag, and de music. Dat's de greatest sight dese eyes ebber saw. An' dey's cum here ter set all de cullud pussons free. De Lord be praised!" and poor old Sarah, quite forgetful of her mistress's presence, began swaying to and fro, chanting a song of her race—

"De Lord, He's cum ter set us free,
An' take us to de haben of bliss,
Way down in de Promised Land."

The twilight had faded into night before Agnes Saumur left her post at the window. The paleness of baffled hope was on her face as she asked herself the one great question ever upon her lips in these troubled days,

"Shall I ever see David Dalton again?"

XI.

HORTON sat looking out from a bay window of his room in the splendid mansion which had been taken for head-quarters. The change from the rough experience of campaigning, where the soldier rarely ever sees the inside of a house except to regret its utter wreck, for the luxury of civilized abodes, affords a contrast which can only be appreciated by an old campaigner. As Horton glanced from the window to the comfortable coal fire glowing in the grate, he wondered that he could ever have thought a camp-fire of pine logs the heighth of luxury. A library of choice books filled one of those curiously carved armoires which are seldom seen except in the palaces of the Old World. On the buffet near were grouped in a singular collection bottles and decanters containing a rare selection of exquisite wines, many of which might, by reason of their many voyages by sea, have been considered old travelers. Others had grown gray with dust and age in the cellars of old magnates, who were prouder of their wines than of their children, and, in many cases, doubtless with good reason. Costly pictures hung upon the wall. Upon a proud pedestal near the window was set that eternal embodiment of grace and beauty, the Venus de Milo. Altogether it was an apartment well suited to its occupant, who was, at the same time, a soldier and an artist.

It was early in January, and the spectacle without was cold and bleak. The wind rustled among the green leaves of the cypress and the pine, whirling the dust and twigs into the box-wood bordered garden-beds, and spreading out the ample folds of the stars and stripes above a regiment quartered in the public square, where the soldiers were building with amazing ingenuity and rapidity their wooden huts for shelter. Groups of soldiers wandered about the streets, curiously regarding the fine houses, and the parks and monuments. Children, guarded by their negro nurses, played among the trees as regardless of the biting air as of the "blood-thirsty" Yankees.

Upon the table lay two letters. One was addressed to Horton by Blauvelt, an artist friend in Boston; the other was his own reply. These are the letters:

"Boston, December 29, 1864.

"Dear Captain,—Every body is talking about the grand March to the Sea. Sherman is a hero! * * * By the way, Horton, we heard some queer stories about you a few weeks ago. It was all about some pretended love affair of yours with a rebel beauty, whom you rescued among those Georgia mountains when she didn't need help, and when you should have been at the front, etc. I was surprised to hear your old friend Gray retailing the story to quite a crowd at Mrs. Somers's reception. What's the matter with this Gray? Did you ever lend him money? Have you crossed him in love? * * * Kate Noble is as grand as ever, and remains the queen. Several of our best young men are paying attentions to her, but they never get beyond a certain point. You must come home, and see what brass buttons can do. By-the-by, when I was looking up your pictures, sketches, etc., which you left in such abominable confusion, scattered about the studio, I found several rough designs, all of which, in one shape or another, represented our friend Kate. I never suspected that you were in love with her, but, since Gray has opened fire, I have thought the matter over. I am sure you will not consider me officious in this matter. Can I do any thing for you, old fellow? Shall I make love to Miss Kate in your behalf? I should like that. Or shall I paint a portrait of Gray in the character of Lawyer Muddle, and send it to the Exhibition? * * * George Inness is painting more gloriously than ever. Gay continues to give us those pure, fresh bits of sea-side scenery, and Hunt knocks off a head now and then, which, could he see it, would make our old Master Couture tumble from his ladder with delight. But what do you care about art, you who are *making* history—who are placing the cap-stone upon the Temple of Liberty, where all people are to come and worship? The wound I received at Gettysburg is slowly healing, but I can never take the field again. Thank Heaven, it does not prevent me from painting.

"Be sure and answer this letter. I have not had a word from you these twelve months.

"BLAUVELT."

"SAVANNAH, January 8, 1864.

"DEAR FRIEND,—I was glad to get your letter, with its details of the folks at home. In regard to that matter about Gray and the stories to which you alluded, I have only one favor to ask. Do not use my name to Kate in any way. If there is one lesson which a true soldier learns in the army more thoroughly than any other, it is to allow acts to speak for themselves, and to pay no regard to calumny. If my friends have not faith enough in me to preserve my honor intact, then let the future take care of itself. No, my dear fellow, do nothing and say nothing about me, especially in the presence of Kate Noble. We shall have but few more campaigns to make. The most terrible battles have been fought. Peace will come soon, and I shall return home. Until then, good-by, old boy.

"Alfred Horton."

The first of these letters Horton had perused for the third time; the reply still lay upon the table unsealed. Evidently there was much in the captain's mind which he had not revealed to his friend. He had been musing over his meerschaum. Blauvelt was entirely forgotten. Only two figures were prominent in his thoughts. The first was Kate Noble's—the central figure in all his pictures of home; the second was Harry Gray's.

"What could Gray's conduct mean?" he asked himself. "If ever a man was bound by every sense of manly honor and of past service to do justice to another, surely Gray is thus bound to me. Does he love Kate? Even then, what necessity for slandering me? Gray does not write me as he used. Bother the whole thing, this comes of being a soldier. If I could have twenty minutes in Boston, I would soon fix this business. But one might as well expect to find patriotism in these secesh women as to get a furlough from the Old Tycoon!"

Then, having forgotten his friend, and thinking only of Kate, he seized a pen and directed the letter intended for Blauvelt to Miss Kate Noble, Mount Vernon Street, Boston. Calling an orderly, he gave him the letter, with instructions to dispatch it by the first mail.

The entrance and exit of the orderly did not interrupt the train of thought which had taken so strong a hold upon Horton's mind. Suddenly the vision which had startled him on the evening after the battle of Fort McAllister flashed upon him, but now he recognized the face of Gray as belonging to the demon of that vision. He identified the exterior features, but these had on that occasion been so disguised with a cruel, heartless sneer, that Horton did not wonder he had failed to discern Gray in that wicked image. But now the likeness was perfect. The vision of that night and the letter from Blauvelt had a miraculous correspondence; to Horton, it almost seemed that the former was a spiritual reflection of a scene that had actually occurred, or else, as if by some mysterious law of mental operation, an element in Gray's character entirely foreign to their friendship hitherto had been suddenly and spontaneously revealed in this wonderful manner. A subsequent event in his military career caused him to wonder less at this singular physiological phenomenon.

E

XII.

HORTON'S speculations were brought to an abrupt termination by a rap at his door.

"Why, Dalton!" he exclaimed, as his old comrade entered the room, "how are you? and where did you come from?"

The answer came in a graver mood, as from one almost weary with life. Dalton sank down into a chair. He thanked his friend, he was well. He had been in the city about three hours. He had traveled day and night from Nashville, which he had left after Hood's defeat.

"I heard," he said, "that you were likely to come out at Savannah."

"Yes, I remember, this was your home. By the way, I have heard about your brother Harold."

"I know the whole story," said Dalton, "and for that reason I did not come to head-quarters at once." His bright eyes flashed with anger. "Harold was in this city only the day before your troops entered. How long he had been here I do not know, but the story told me by that rebel prisoner in the mountains was in the main correct. After I escaped from Savannah, Harold was conscripted. His safest means of escape was to go with the army. He tried to get away, was captured, court-martialed, and sentenced to be shot, but was reprieved on condition that he would volunteer to enter the ranks again. Whether he submitted I do not know, but in the mean while he was taken down with the fever, and was removed to the hospital here, where he remained until the day before the evacuation, when he was dragged away with the fugitive army. I am told by the citizens here that they can get him exchanged, and I have come to see the general about it."

"You have only to tell him your story," said Horton, who heartily sympathized with his friend's distress, "and he will go any length to assist you."

As Horton had anticipated, the general listened attentively to the whole story, and at once gave the major the authority to effect an exchange of rebel prisoners for his brother.

Dalton forgot his own fatigue as, with the papers for his brother's release, he sallied forth out of the house arm-in-arm with his friend.

"This is not the Savannah which you left four years ago, I imagine," remarked Horton, as they passed the old United States barracks, whose windows and doorways were crowded with soldiers in blue, while a band of music under the windows of the post-commandant were playing national airs.

"By the way," he added, "how do your old acquaintances receive you?"

"To tell you the truth, Horton, since I came back I have had neither the time nor the inclination to think of any thing else but my brother. As for the people here, although my personal appearance has not changed much, yet few would recognize me in my uniform."

Dalton's physique had altered far more than he supposed. His eye had become more stern and fixed, not merely by sighting cannon amid the smoke and thunder of many battle-fields, but by an inward purpose which had grown to be inflexible, and which seemed now almost triumphant. His mouth had little of its old expression of gentleness, and his whole face was more rigid and immovable. There was no restlessness of look; no fluctuating waves of passion ruffled the face, which had been overmastered by a calm which only those could have understood who had witnessed the terrible struggles through which it had been attained. As he walked, his look was straight ahead; there was no hesitation in his steps; he knew only duty, and therefore dealt only with instant decision.

"But why should I desire to revive old acquaintances here?" continued Dalton. "There is no bond of sympathy between them and myself. They hate the old Union, which I revere, and for which I would die. They look upon me as denationalized. In their sense of the word, doubtless I am. But I love the South not less than they, though I do not agree with them as to its proper glory and its legitimate hope. No, Horton, they will only come to me to ask for help. The fight is nearly over, and I can see the despair of defeat already written in their faces. I can not triumph over them. I do not come to witness their humiliation, and I shall avoid—"

The sudden vision of Agnes Saumur it was which had interrupted Dalton's concluding remark. With a heart beating with wild joy, she had recognized him first, and was hastening to meet him. The hopes, the prayers, the loving longings of wistful years were now to be realized at last. One only comfort there had been for her all along—her faith in him. His self-sacrificing devotion to duty had been also to her a grand example—a guiding star in the darkness. She had waited for his coming, how fondly and how anxiously! And here he was. She could now prove to him, with many a gentle word and caress, how she had loved him all the while, and what a rich harvest she had gathered during these long years—a harvest of his own sowing—and her heart thrilled with exulting pride as she saw him. His blue uniform seemed to fitly clothe the vision for which she had so patiently waited; it was to her, also, the emblem of law and liberty.

"Well," said Horton, waiting for his friend to finish his sentence.

"Let us turn this way," replied Dalton. "But it is too late. She has seen us. I would rather not have met her, but it might as well come now as at any other time."

Agnes's quick eye saw that Dalton had recognized her, and that he would have turned the other way. His last words, too, had reached her ear. It was hard on the instant to take into her consciousness the thought that he really wished to shun her. She did not remember the last time they were face to face, and how she had then met his impassioned pleadings for love and sympathy, and how much had passed since then. She was conscious only of the new joy thrilling her every sense—of present love and uprising hope. If she had hesitated longer —if she had tried to read the face upon which she looked as in a dream, she would have found there no answer either for love or hope, but a repellant wave which would have beaten her back upon the forlorn coast of her immediate past. But she did not thus read. How could she, when she was self-inspired— when she was thus irresistibly borne away by the current that carried her out from the desolate waste which her life had been ranging toward him.

And so Agnes pressed forward, her eyes seeking his with that faith and fullness of expectant love which one sees in the upturned faces of Perugino's adoring angels.

But—and she, poor child, *must* see it now—there was scarcely recognition in the stern gaze which met her own, and what there was was like the light which momentarily flashes across the rain-clouds, and leaves them again as dark and forbidding as before. Before she had even spoken he had passed on.

"Good heavens! Dalton, what is the meaning of this singular performance?" asked his friend, who had witnessed this earnest appeal and its terrible repulse.

"Do not ask me to explain, Horton. You will not misunderstand me, I am sure, but there are sufficient reasons why this encounter should pass as if it had never happened."

Dalton's voice trembled with ill-concealed emotion. Could it be that the calm which he had won for himself, and which almost seemed immovable and eternal, was but a frail possession after all? Could it be that a trouble conquered could still haunt the conqueror, and that a struggle once fought out to its bitter close could repeat itself upon so slight an occasion? And what virtue, then, is there in decision, if, after all, the issues which Fate ordains refuse to be decided by any human arbitration? What if Fate reserves decisions to herself alone?

But the two officers had reached their destination, and, answering the salute of a sentinel at the door, passed into the house of a citizen who had promised to procure the exchange of Harold Dalton.

XIII.

AGNES SAUMUR rushed wildly, blindly along the streets, unmindful of the wondering gaze of passers-by, deaf to the strains of martial music which filled the air, home, home, home, to hide her face from human sight, to weep tears of anguish, to cry out aloud in her agony of grief. She knew David Dalton. The stern, unyielding face, still looking upon her, spoke more than words. "He does not love me longer." They had changed places. She saw this now. After her repulse, she could remember how, four years ago, she had beaten him back from her. And time had done its work with them both. Her it had changed, while it softened; him it had changed also, but in a different way. The shadow which she had just seen in all its darkness had grown out of the shadow which she had raised herself at their last meeting.

She pressed her almost bursting temples with her

hands, as if to drive the vision from her sight. But it would not leave her. The very intensity and unchanging loyalty of his early love gave her nothing to hope as against his indifference now. If it were the despite of petty revenge, there might be hope. But Dalton's nature had no such meanness. He could not deceive her. His high sense of honor would not let him assume a sentiment which did not exist in his heart. He did not love her.

"Oh, if he could know what I have suffered!" Through her trials and persecutions he had been the pillar of fire by night and the cloud by day. And now, in sight of the promised land, she was left to die. And she cried for death. Great sobs came welling up thick and fast, and it seemed as if her life would free itself in tears. At last her tired heart found rest in sleep; but still she sobbed in sleep, and hot tears trickled through the closed lids, as, when a stone is cast into a lake, disturbing its calm reflections of bank, and tree, and sky, the bubbles rise and break upon the surface in mute protest long after the surface has sunk to rest."

XIV.

"HAVE you been deceiving me?" inquired Dalton of Mr. Harding, the citizen who had engaged to secure Harold's release, and who had appeared at head-quarters in answer to the major's summons. "This paper is returned to me with an indorsement declaring that my brother is a deserter from the Confederate army, and will in no event be given up to the Federal authorities."

Several days had elapsed, and the messenger had returned with this answer.

"I assure you, Major Dalton, I had every reason to believe that I could effect this exchange. I have influence with the general commanding the Confederate army. There must be some extraordinary, some underhand work here which has defeated our efforts. But, sir, it has been no fault of mine," Mr. Harding continued, as Dalton paced the room to and fro, disappointed, angry, and heart-sick. Almost within touch of his hand, and his brother was lost again. Perhaps at this moment the poor sick man was dragging his feeble limbs along rough roads, or sighing away his last breath in some wretched prison hospital. The thought was maddening.

"Mr. Harding," he said, suddenly turning upon that individual, "I have said nothing to you of the injuries you inflicted upon me and mine when the war broke out. I have the power to-day, and you are helpless. I do not retaliate, but I do not forget. I never struck at a fallen foe. I do not wish to harm you; but, Mr. Harding, if I find that you have played me false in this matter of my poor brother, you shall occupy the filthy hole where he has dragged out a long, miserable existence; you shall eat the food which was given him to eat; and if in any degree you suffer the pangs he suffered, it will be more punishment than you can bear."

As Harding left Major Dalton, his was probably the uneasiest mind in the city of Savannah.

Dalton gave way for an instant to the reaction which succeeded his mortifying pleasure; but, as his large brown eyes were fixed upon the rebel indorsement, as he sat by his table with his hands clenched and his brow knit with unconquerable resolve, it was plain that he had no surrender to make, and that he would at any cost pursue to the end the work which he had undertaken.

An unusual turmoil at the door aroused him. He could hear the sound of voices on the sidewalk gradually approaching nearer and into the hall.

"There is no use talking, old woman, you can't go in there. The major's orders are not to admit any one," cried the orderly.

"Dat's all berry well for common folks, but I tell ye I nussed Massa Dalton in dese hans, an' I'd like ter see ef yer perwents me from finin' out Massa Dalton arter foar years is pass an' gone away."

"I'll take your name, but you can't go in until the major says so," replied the orderly by way of compromise.

Dalton was at the door. "It's all right; let her come in," he said.

In a moment old Sarah was in the room. At first she could not give vent in words to her love and reverence for her master's son—her own favorite of all the family, but, dropping on her knees, she threw her arms about him, and then grasped both his hands in hers, and held them to her face. Then, lifting her arms, she prayed with tearful fervor—

"Oh, de Almighty God, de Lord Jesus be praised, my Massa David is right dar alibe afore my ole eyes.

De prayers of poor Sarah is heard in de mansions ob bliss, an' he is come back ter der ole home."

Dalton's eyes moistened. Every memory of his youth and early manhood was associated with this good old loving creature, and, next to Harold, she was nearer to him than any other person in the city of his childhood.

"Well, Sarah, I am glad to see your kind old face again. You must tell me all about yourself. Of course you have been well cared for since I left. Mr. Bright promised me you should be."

"Lor bress me, Massa Dalton—but youse an ossifer now—Major Dalton. Major—dat soun's well. How han'some you looks in dat ar blue coat wid de bright buttons. La! you is han'some, de Lord knows dat," and Sarah stood at seeing distance and surveyed the major with admiration. "Who'd a tort, mas—major, dat youse come back here, arter all, a grea-at big ossifer, wid a sojer at de door ter keep watch? De Lord be praised youse come back!" and, her wonder appeased, Sarah again broke out into demonstrations of ecstatic pleasure.

After a while Dalton was able to reduce her to something like order.

"I'se not bin wid Massa Bright, but dey's bin Union all de time," she said. "So soon as ebber you get away, dat bressed angel, Miss Agnes, come an' tuk me ter her house, an' dar I'se bin ebber since. Ef she'd a bin my own chile, I couldn't a bin car'd fur more."

"That was very kind of Miss Saumur," said Dalton, rather coldly.

"But dat isn't de commencement of what she done. It's nuthin' but good works all de way 'long, arter she'd separated from de sesesh. An' she did hav orful quar'ls wid dese peoples, when she'd defen' de ole Union, and said sesesh was a sin. One day her uncle died wid a fever he tuck at de war. Den she left all dese peoples, an' sit alone. Ebbery day when de Yankee pris'ners pass troo heyar—dey come from Charleston, an' dey put dem all down in de sidewalk in Liberty Street 'fore dey put dem in de cars to send way off ter Milten and An'sonville. Oh! Massa Dalton, de orful sights us see ebbery dey, ebbery day—dere dese wounded men, an' sick, trown out ob de cars like hogs, an' den Miss Agnes go roun' 'mong dem wid a basket full ob nice tings ter eat. She look like an angel come right down from hebben, wid her big black eyes so full ob light, an' her face white as de cotton-fiel's. You know, Massa David, she like an angel!" and the old negress peered into the face of Dalton as if she would fain interpret his thoughts.

"Well, go on, Sarah," was his only answer, while with his hand he shaded his face from the blaze of the burning lightwood which flared and crackled in the large fireplace.

"Ah! I 'member well, one day," continued old Sarah, as if talking to herself, "dere was a man wid torn clo's; his legs wos jes' like cornstalks, dey so small an' hard; de har all drop off ob his head; his eyes sunk way in his eyebrows, wid great black spots un'erneath. Miss Agnes gib him piece ob bread, an' when he put it in his mouf de blood run from his teef an' make de bread all red, an' den Miss Agnes cry like a chile, an' den de pris'ner cry dreful, an' I cry a heap. One day de guard tell Miss Agnes ter go way an' let de dam Yankees die. Lor' bress me, Massa David, you'd orter seen how de sparks flew right out ob Miss Agnes's eyes. De guard not dare say 'nudder word. Bime-by she heerd tell dat Massa Harol was in de hosp'tal pris'n down by de railroad, an' fur weeks an' mon's she went dar, a-nussin' him like's ef she'd bin his sister. She couldn't do 'nuff fur yer sick brudder, an' many's de time I heerd him bress her, while wid his eyes as blue as de firm'ment he'd foller her about dat hole. She tinks a heep ob you, Massa David," cried the old woman, suddenly advancing, and with the familiarity of the old family nurse, she laid her long bony hand on the major's arm.

Dalton made no answer, but closed his eyes, as if to shut out the picture she had drawn.

"Yes, Massa David, yer'll let yer ole mammy speak ter yer. Las' Monday week agone—no, 'twas Tuesday—Miss Agnes come home an' ran right ter her room, an' den I heerd such cryin' and groanin', and she talk out loud ter herself, an' I was afeerd ter go in dere until, bime-by, dere wos no noise, an' I fin' her on de floor, her face all sorrowful wid de tears, but she sleep like a baby. She nebber hab lef' dat room since dat day."

Before she had finished her story Dalton's arms had fallen upon the table, and his head rested upon them, and thus he remained, when Sarah left him, feeling that she should say no more, and silently stole from the room.

Hours passed, and still Major Dalton had not moved from his position. Rigidly did he examine himself, and weigh every thought and motive. A thousand memories of old days of love in the past came thronging into court in passionate appeal. To give his life for her happiness would be a poor compensation for her grand heroism, her tender devotion to his comrades and to his brother. Could he mistake the world of confident, expectant love which filled her eyes on the day of their meeting? What right had he to refuse this noble offering? He should be a king among men to wear so rich a crown. What grander aim? What higher duty? What nobler aspiration than to devote his best life to this noble girl? And then, in spite of all, came back upon him the terrible thought, crushing with remorseless hand these eloquent but subtle fallacies:

"Oh no, I will not deceive myself—I will not lie to her. Four years ago I asked her to be my wife; that was to me the crucial hour, deciding all. She refused me, and from that moment she passed out of my love as if she had never been. No, I will not deceive myself—I will not lie to her. I do not love Agnes Saumur."

XV.

IT was with a sad, hopeless heart that Agnes Saumur, yielding to the earnest solicitation of Mrs. Bright, took her place in that lady's carriage.

"You are not well, my child," said Mrs. Bright, as she wrapped a shawl about her friend. "What ails you? Here you have been shut up in your room for weeks. The fresh air will cheer you. There is nothing like sunshine for invalids. We will have a pleasant drive to Thunderbolt, and I know you will enjoy it."

The sun shone pleasantly enough as they drove down Liberty Street, and out upon the shell road—once a broad, smooth avenue, now cut up by the passage of heavy army wagons. As they passed through the massive fortification and over the wooden bridge which spanned the wide ditch, and out upon the open plain, they could see the gray and purple clouds in the south working swiftly and restlessly northward. Then the wind shifted to the east, and came cold and bleak, penetrating and chilling the blood. Very soon the sun gave up the contest for the mastery, and hid itself behind the mists and scudding clouds.

"Drive to Bonaventura, and leave me there. You can take me up on your way back," said Agnes. The change in the weather was quite in consonance with Agnes's mood, and she resolved to visit the tomb of her parents, perhaps for the last time, for during her illness she had revolved the possibilities of her future life. In Savannah she could not and would not remain. Every association with the place was repulsive to her. She had cousins in New York who had generously urged her to make her future home with them. She was independent of others so far as pecuniary considerations were concerned, and she had resolved to accept her cousins' invitation. Perhaps, under other circumstances and associations, some new sphere of usefulness would open, where she could wear out her heart's pain.

XVI.

PERHAPS in all the world there is not a more remarkable burial-place for the dead than Bonaventura. When, centuries ago, the Spanish adventurers, navigating the creeks and rivers which divide the sea-coast into main land and barren island, came suddenly upon this luxurious growth of live-oak-trees clustered upon the river-bank, and then, in their joyous enthusiasm, cried out "bonaventura,"* they little imagined that it was one day to serve as a cemetery of a great city near, or that underneath the branches of the wide-spreading trees where they pitched their silken tents there would rise monuments covering the ashes of their children's children.

In every direction in this great cemetery long avenues traverse the forest, whose gnarled, sturdy branches have for centuries woven a cathedral arch above, the avenues themselves extending away from the beholder until they are lost in the distance.

* Good luck.

At no season of the year does the sunlight enter here. A thick, gray mist, rising from malarious swamp and fen, gathers among the foliage, matting its graceful forms, and enwrapping the giant limbs as with a death-shroud.

As Agnes entered this gloomy abode of the dead, a nameless horror crept over her, which, while it was a fit reflex of her own mood, seemed also a presentiment of coming evil. The drooping, pendulous moss seemed to embrace her in its snaky coils; it clung to her hair, and swept over her pallid face. The murky shadows of the forest to her vivid imagination assumed weird and fantastic forms of human shape, swaying to and fro as if to beckon her in among the time-stained tombs. No sound disturbed this fearful solitude except the sighing and moaning wind. No face of man greeted her as, with timid steps, she glided along the avenues, past ruined monuments, past broken tablets, the obliterated records of the forgotten dead, and then out from these grim shadows to the river's bank, to her mother's tomb, where she prostrated herself, clasping the cold earth with a great cry of relief and of passionate appeal, as if the form laid there these many years would then, as in the days of her childhood, take her darling child to her bosom to calm her fears, to assuage her grief, to soothe her to rest. The mute earth, that drank her fast-falling tears, gave back no answer to her prayers. With straining eyes she gazed out across the ruin, and over the dreary waste of marshes toward the sea, but a thick veil of fog and mist obscured from her sight that sublime element of eternity. With fitful gusts the wind swept through the weeds and grasses; the sky, now black with clouds, looked threateningly upon her, and, turn which way she would, repellant nature threw her back upon herself.

She was startled from her sad thoughts by the distant sounds of drums beating the long roll of a funeral march, and then the strains of a band of music floated through the aisles of the forest. As the sounds came nearer, she could distinguish the plaintive melody of the Thulee song. And then a regiment of soldiers appeared in sight, with arms reversed, followed by pall-bearers carrying a coffin upon a platform draped with flags, and following this came a group of officers. The cortége filed off to the right, and halted at a new-made grave. Agnes could see the coffin lowered into the earth; the sharp report of muskets paying the salute of honor reached her ears, and then, the last ceremonies finished, the soldiers again fell into line, marching away with quick step, while the group of officers silently separated in one or another direction.

To the excited mind of Agnes, these obsequies, which passed so quickly, appeared like the fragment of a tragedy in which she had herself been an actor—a figure of her own troubled life. This brave soldier had marched many a weary journey, had encountered many perils, and now had gone quietly to his rest in the hour of sublime victory. Had she not also made the grand campaign? But had she thus conquered, and could she glory in a rest like his? Could this intense love for David Dalton be buried thus peacefully? She gazed out over the melancholy marshes, and into the mournful mists, as if the shifting, fickle spirits of the air could give her answer.

There was now a lull in the wind, which had been gradually increasing from the northeast. Agnes heard the sound of footsteps, and, turning, saw Dalton approaching, followed by a soldier leading two horses. It was too late to avoid a meeting, for he had already recognized, and was advancing toward her with rapid strides. The young girl's heart almost ceased to beat—a sensation of suffocation overcame her. With a nervous grasp she tore the collar from her neck, but this gave no relief. The light passed from her eyes, and she sank upon the ground. When she came to herself again she was resting in Dalton's arms. Oh, the thankful, gentle rest, the peace, the happiness of that brief moment of awakening consciousness! She was only too content to lie there; but Dalton's voice aroused her to the cruel reality. Those were not the familiar tones, trembling with the music of love, but a soldier's voice, cold and inflexible—the voice of command.

"That will do, orderly," he said; "she is coming to her senses. Fasten my horse to the tree yonder, then ride as quickly as you can to Savannah. Take the grand avenue on your way up to the city, and hail the first carriage you meet. It is possible you may find the one this lady came in. Make haste!"

The clatter of hoofs died away in the forest, and the estranged lovers were alone. With a gentle touch Dalton smoothed away the hair, and kissed the pale face which lay half-buried in his cloak. He at once divined the grief which had brought her to her mother's grave. He knew then, as never before, the depth of her love for him, and he bent over her, crying out in his compassion,

"Agnes, Agnes, so loving, so impetuous."

There was exceeding tenderness in his voice, but it did not deceive Agnes for a moment. Love, in a delicate nature like hers is wonderfully sensitive. It detects and analyzes the lightest word with absolute certainty; it translates each look and tone into its proper language. There are no infidelities in the chemistry of love. Agnes accepted the truth with all its bitterness, and yet his words fell upon her wounded spirit with healing balm. The tears forced themselves through her long eyelashes, and she pressed his hand to her lips and against her throbbing heart.

Dalton made no effort to restrain the sobs which shook her frail form. A tempest of contending emotions struggled within him until his strong nature bent and swayed as helplessly as the tough oak wrenched by the gale on the river bank. As he looked down into that fair face, the loving-kindness of his gentler self found voice, and for the moment the memory of his neglected love came back to him with thrilling power.

"Agnes, dear Agnes, do not sob so; it breaks my heart. I will be all in all to you. Oh, Agnes, forgive me the pain I have caused you. But it is all past now. You shall never know sorrow any more."

Agnes did not at once answer his loving, soothing words. For a while she shut out all sense but that of loving. But then slowly and reluctantly she withdrew herself from his embrace, while she yet held fast his hands in hers. Then the grandeur of her unselfish woman's soul expanded in earnest utterances, pleading as against herself.

"David Dalton, I have loved you. I love you now with all my heart and soul—perhaps you will never know how deeply and intensely. But, oh! David, forgive me, I will not take you at your generous word. You do not love me now, I fear, as you did—"

"Agnes!"

"Do not speak now. I ought to have anticipated this years ago. It was my own weakness, my crime which drove you from me, but indeed I forgot all that in the selfishness of my love. I remembered too much of all that was good and noble in you. I was too happy in these memories; they kindled into life a pride in our dear country. This love for you, David, has sustained me through bitter trials. My battles have not been fought on the fields where you have contended so nobly, but they have been severe, and, like yours, they have resulted in victory. But I owe all to you. After I met you the other day I saw that I was nothing to you. Yet in the after hours, in the silence of despair, I would have taken you at your word. But, David, this is the impulse of your generous heart. You do not love me as you must love the woman who is to be your wife."

Her voice fluttered, and the words came brokenly from her white lips.

"Do not think I blame you. The current of our feelings is sometimes beyond our control. I could scarcely have expected that in your case the event would have been otherwise than it has been. But to-day over this sacred grave I have struggled with myself, and all in vain. Your own nobleness of nature has given me a strength which was denied to myself. I ought not, David, and I can not be your wife."

Then she released herself entirely, and stood alone, beautiful in her self-immolation and with her divine resignation.

"Agnes," said Dalton, "could you look into my heart, you would see how supremely I honor you. God grant that I may live to prove to you that I love you. Let us have faith that we have both been saved for some better fate."

There was a pleading earnestness in his eyes which caused Agnes to tremble with uncontrollable emotion, and she covered her face with her hands, and would have fled from him.

"I know that I am rougher, harder than in the

old days," he continued. "Have patience with me. Perhaps—"

"Oh, David," she interrupted, "do not speak in that way. I am bewildered. You must help me to be strong. Thank God, they have come at last!"

As Agnes spoke, Mrs. Bright's carriage whirled rapidly out of the avenue. Dalton placed her tenderly within the carriage. There was a pressure of the hand, and once again Agnes Saumur and David Dalton were parted.

XVII.

INSTRUCTING his orderly to follow the carriage to Savannah, and to render the party any assistance which might be needed, Dalton mounted his horse and rode slowly toward a series of massive fortifications which covered the river bank. At this point, where there was a sharp bend in the river, the Confederate engineers had constructed broad traverses, which protected numerous redoubts, and which were, in their turn, covered in the rear by an extensive bastioned fort. The muzzles of ponderous cannon looked out from earthen embrasures upon the lofty parapet. Here an old-fashioned sixty-four-pounder was dismounted from its carriage; behind an embankment, half buried in the sand, lay a big-throated mortar; iron balls, canister, and shells were scattered about just as they had been left by the garrison a few weeks ago.

Dismounting from his horse, Major Dalton threw his reins over a broken rammer thrust into the earth, and walked into a huge embrasure, which, from its height, its earthy material, and scientific construction, almost entirely protected its defenders from the fire of ships approaching from the sea. In these interior lines of defense the Confederates had learned a lesson as to the incapacity of stone walls from their dearly-bought experience at Fort Pulaski. As Dalton gazed up and down the river bank, he could see rising from the earth these huge mounds of sand, mounted with embrasured guns, pointing in every direction, but all concentrating upon that one point in the stream where the attacking ship must expose her broadside to their annihilating fire.

"A few weeks ago," thought the major, "and that splendid ship could not have ridden so securely at her anchor, within reach of these guns, as she does to-day. These powerful engines of destruction are harmless enough now. A few days since, and they kept a fleet at bay."

Dejected and unhinged, the major's mind seemed to rest in sad harmony with all this wreck and ruin. The spirit of man is ever bound in close relations to the earth. The exterior appearance of nature influences his being, moulding it into good shapes or ill, moving it to joy or sorrow. These affinities or correspondences act and react in obedience to great laws, and with as much certainty and regularity as those which have been more clearly defined and subjected to absolute rules.

Why should the heart leap with gladness when the sun shines and the golden clouds ride gayly across the sky, while the breeze bends with gentle force the boughs, and rustles the leaves of the forest-trees?

Why should the soul sink with sadness in the autumn days, when leaden skies overhang the earth, and the chill wind whistles among the limbs of trees that are gaunt and bare?

As Dalton looked into himself, he saw a spiritual counterpart of this machinery of power lying useless and helpless about him. It was only yesterday that he was strong to will, to resist, and to achieve. He felt within himself the springs of power—a reserved strength which could assert itself upon provocation; but for the moment he was paralyzed; and as the major shielded his body from the wind which came howling from the ocean, flirting in his face now and then spiteful splashes of rain, he recalled the immediate details of the scene with Agnes, which but an hour ago had passed so quickly.

"How came this weakness? Why this sense of humiliation, unless he had been untrue to himself?" Again he asked himself, with terrible earnestness,

"Do I love Agnes, after all? Could I ask myself such a question, or should I dread to ask, if I really loved her? What has become of the passion of four years ago? Into what channel has it run? Has it only been dormant the while, or is it lost forever?" In the noble qualities which had been developed by sorrowful experience in Agnes, he could scarcely recognize the woman he had once loved. She was all she had ever been, but how much more! The latent possibilities for good or evil are greater in women than in men, partly because of the infinite susceptibility which is in them, and partly because of the secluded lives they lead. Woman is a never-ceasing mystery, which man had best thankfully accept and despair of divining. But Dalton was not reasoning—if his chaotic mind was then capable of reasoning—from the stand-point which Agnes had taken. He was rather fighting a battle with himself. Dalton possessed in an eminent degree that characteristic called "chivalric," too often misunderstood, or falsely attributed to absurd bombast, but which undoubtedly belonged to many a Southron, and was founded in a noble spirit of manly self-sacrifice.

"Yes," he said to himself, "I can never give my love to any woman but her. I will devote my life to her. She will not—she can not reject the offering."

XVIII.

IT was late when the major returned to his quarters. He found an officer awaiting him with imperative orders for his instant departure upon important service.

"When do we start?"

"The steamer, which takes up a party of pioneers, is waiting for you at the wharf. It should start in half an hour."

The major's face flushed at the thought of dereliction, and in a moment the affectionate impulses of his nature yielded to the habit of action and to the requirements of soldierly discipline. The mission with which he was intrusted was one of great importance. He saw that he was the *avant courier* in the opening of a new and grand campaign. The sublime scope of the new movement thrilled him. He saw its gigantic plan, and, though its successful execution was obscured by a thousand obstructions and perils, its success would decide the war of the rebellion.

But after all, in the midst of these bright pictures rose up the pale, sad face of Agnes, with sorrowful eyes, appealing to him. See her he must before entering upon this expedition.

"I will be with you in a few minutes. Wait for me here, captain," and Major Dalton hurried upon his errand.

He did not hope to overcome the doubts or the resolves of Agnes, but he was determined to give her assurance of hopes entertained by himself, and of his faith in their future.

"Well, dar you ar, Massa David. I tort yer'd be comin'," was the salutation of the old nurse Sarah at the door. "Yer want to see Miss Agnes, I s'pose. But, Massa David, dat ar chile's not well. She suffers a heap. She tort yer'd be comin', an' she told me dat she couldn't bar to see yer nohow, an' she gib me dis letter fur yer ter read bime-by, not h'yar in dis house, but arterward, somewhar."

"But you must tell Miss Agnes that I am ordered away—that I leave in a few moments, and that I wish to see her only for an instant."

"It's no use, Massa David. Dat chile is sick in her bed. Yer can't see her. It's right hard, Massa

David, but it's no use," and Sarah wiped the perspiration from her bronzed forehead. To refuse "Massa David" was to her a new experience, and to thrust him away from a relation in whose success her own heart was bound up was too much for the old servant, and there were tears in her kindly eyes as she placed her hand upon his shoulder and reiterated,

"It's no use, Massa David; yer mus' go right away."

"Well, well, tell your mistress I will return again," said the major, as, securing the letter, he hurried from the house.

It was past midnight when he read Agnes's letter by the moonlight which at intervals broke through the masses of black clouds, lighting up the deck of the steamer. And these were the words which he read, steeped in the bitterness of sorrow:

"The tears are falling fast. I can not keep them back and write what must be written, for, if you were with me now, I could not speak these words. Oh! the unbearable sorrow to say Good-by, and forever.

"No, David, we must not see each other again. I could convince you that this separation is for the best, but you must comprehend it all for yourself. Do not attempt to persuade me, nor yourself, from the only path we ought to pursue. You will not regret this by-and-by. I fly from you—from myself. The Agnes Saumur of the past no longer exists. There are solemn duties before you—to your brother, to your country. Forgive me the pain I have caused you. Farewell. AGNES."

Out of the nobility of loving came these tearful words. It was not that her pride revolted against Dalton. She refused to permit him to make a sacrifice for what he believed would be her happiness. She trampled self under foot, and stood between him and his generous impulses.

But her mediation was unavailing. The conflict in Dalton's soul had already begun. It was not the old conflict renewed. Duty, now disarmed, was no longer an element in the field. Honor, which sometimes takes the guise of love, had here no place. All shams and pretenses were cast aside. The life which scorned love when love could no longer meet the emergencies of life, now swayed toward a loving presence, which was stronger than naked duty only because it was transformed into the divinity of self-immolation and of absolute self-renunciation.

And the major stretched himself upon the steamer's deck, vaguely yearning for some light to guide him through this labyrinth; thankful for the silence, broken only by the smothered breathings of the steam monster underneath him; thankful for the night which hid his face and thought from human observation; unmindful of the spectral cloud-shadows chasing each other across the watery waste and the misty main land; unmindful of the gloomy forest opening its giant arms of darkness to receive these shadows; unconscious of the destiny which Fate, with subtle fingers, was weaving about him.

XIX.

MAJOR DALTON, after a week had passed, found himself still on the bank of the Savannah River, contending stoutly with the turbid, rushing waters. The relentless flood tore in pieces the canvas pontoon boats, uplifted and carried away bridges, tossing, twisting, and sweeping away the corduroy roads; wagons in the causeways, wagons in the fields, wagons every where struggled for a time, and then settled in the mud, and were finally abandoned. The mules waded, and plunged, and swam until their heavy heads and long ears carried them beneath the all-absorbing waters.

It is wellnigh impossible to convey to the mind of a stranger the nature of the country on the left bank of the Savannah. Said a Confederate general officer, "It would have taken our army, under the most favorable auspices, three years to have built the roads over which Sherman marched to the Salkahatchie."

And to-day, as those who accomplished these wonderful feats of patience and ingenuity look back upon their triumph over apparently insurmountable obstacles, they wonder at themselves, and thank God that they were not left to starve or drown in the swamps and rice-fields.

Meanwhile the brigade which had been sent with Major Dalton had become a division. By one means or another the troops were arriving rapidly, and the division grew into a corps, and then an army. It was the first scene in the second stage of the Grand March.

In the struggle between man and the elements, Nature in the main has had the worst of it, but now and then she asserts herself, and human forces must stand still or give way. The left wing of Sherman's army stood still for a while on the higher southern bank of the river in January, 1865, while the waters with defiant, drunken glee ran riotous over the land.

Major Dalton, with the rest, watched and waited, held to his post by the obligations of duty. But he was not impatient. These hours of rest were not fruitless. The finer sensibilities of his nature were gaining strength. There was springing into life that richer and more generous growth of love which preludes its "second harvest."

XX.

AT this moment, while Dalton stands upon the bank of the river, self-questioning, at Savannah, an ocean steam-ship swings slowly into the stream. On her quarter-deck, separated from the group of passengers, there sits, clinging to the rail, a gentle, sad-eyed woman. Fast-falling tears find their way down her pale face as she waves adieu to an old negress weeping and moaning among the idle spectators on the pier. And then, with listless indifference, the lady upon the quarter-deck hears the paddles which beat against the yielding waters. The great vessel moves among the throng of shipping away from the noble warehouses, past cotton-presses and steam-mills, past the great city; gathering speed with the outflowing tide, she darts through the narrow, dangerous pass, avoiding the iron-peaked timbers planted in the stream to pierce to destruction the Yankee fleets. The lady gives little heed to

Fort Jackson, frowning down upon them with its iron-throated sentinels. Her eyes are fixed upon the spires of the church under whose shadow she had glided—oh, so joyously!—from childhood. into womanhood.

The ship speeds swiftly on past signal-station and ruined earth-work, past sunken ships whose skeletons rise from the sullen waters as if clutching, with phantom fingers, for help which can not come, past sand-spits, where sea-birds, silent and sad, sat resting from their battle with ocean storms, until the city is now but a checkered patch upon the gray horizon. And yet the ship moved on, giving wide berth to the treacherous bar where the light-house stands, which, four years ago, by treacherous hands had been robbed of its warning signal. And now she plunges into the white-capped waves, outriders to old Neptune's chariot. The distant city has faded into the clouds, the church spire is a thin, black line against the sky, and at length even that has vanished. Pulaski, with its encasements of brick and stone, sinks now into the gray and purple distance. The martello tower on lone Tybee, time-defying and mysterious relic of some ancient people, crumbles among the yellow sands, and all that may be seen of the solid earth is a spectral boundary-line, which is soon swallowed up by the leaping waves, crimson-crested by the setting sun.

A film covers the lady's eye, coming between her and this fading vision. The ship has gone out upon the broad ocean, and Agnes Saumur has bidden adieu to home, to love, and to David Dalton.

XXI.

ONE day the rain ceased falling, the waters began to subside, and the low lands to appear in sight again, and then brigade and division began to cross the river, and haul out upon all the available roads. Every possible avenue of travel was made use of. Commanders were instructed to take one and another route, to march upon separate roads in so far as they could be found, but they were all to concentrate at a designated point.

And then commenced the work of the staff corps. At such times, in the actual movement of troops, the officers of the line are occupied with the care of their immediate commands. Their duties are important, but they are well defined. It is far different with the staff corps. The staff officers are the arms and legs of the general, and in some cases in this war they were his brains also. No duty can be more arduous than theirs when the army is in actual motion through the enemy's country. The staff officer must be familiar with the details of the organization and the work they have to perform. Of all the three branches of the service, military topography should be at his fingers' ends.

The staff corps in the Union army was anomalous in its condition. In most cases it was not provided for in the regulations. At one time it was supposed that a position on a general's staff was what the soldier's call a "soft thing;" but that idea vanished at length, as more of the truth was known.

Perhaps no army ever came into existence which so much needed an efficient staff corps as did the Army of the Union, and certainly no army ever created one so rapidly. The civil engineer on the Western prairie, who dropped his chain and compass and took up the sword, in a month's experience could lay out a line of fortifications as well, and build a bridge as quickly and as strongly as his brother officer who had left West Point at the head of his class. The Boston mechanic, who hung up his apron and enlisted in Nims's Battery, in a short time knew as much about gunnery, and the way shot and shell were made, as did the chief of the Ordnance Bureau; while the adjutant general's department found its wisest, clearest heads and nimblest hands from among those who had served in the shipping and counting-house. All of which is not cited as an argument against military education in the schools, but as an evidence of the extraordinary adaptability of the American people to fill the strange positions to which they were so suddenly called.

XXII.

IT was in the exercise of his duties as inspector of his corps that our old acquaintance, Colonel Leveridge, accompanied by Major Dalton, was reconnoitring the country one day in the early part of February.

Dalton, having fulfilled the duty which had called him from Savannah, was seeking an opportunity to rejoin his head-quarters, which at the time were moving northward from Beaufort with the right wing of the army. For several hours Dalton and Colonel Leveridge had been vainly searching for a road which was clearly enough marked upon the map of South Carolina, but which their most patient endeavors had not succeeded in locating in fact. Either this highway was in disuse in A.D. 1865, or it had been overflowed. So they floundered along toward a group of negro huts, whose angular form broke the straight horizon line separating the distant rice-fields from the red sky.

"There must have been troops there, either the rebels or ours, for that column of smoke indicates house-burning," said Dalton.

Leveridge quickly raised his field-glass to his eyes, while the party halted.

"There is quite a large body of men going into camp. Yes; and I can see off to the left a train of wagons slowly moving up to the place," replied Leveridge. "They are our soldiers, too, for I can distinguish a crowd of men with blue coats gathered around a camp-fire."

The party pressed on, and, as they neared the place, they could see squads of soldiers running hither and thither, carrying off rails, boards, and straw to be used for fire and bedding. The smoking timbers were tumbled among the ruined foundations of what appeared once to have been a large house. In front of a row of negro cabins were groups of black people standing and staring in silent wonder at this sudden irruption of strangers. Near a large camp-fire stood several officers.

"I declare," exclaimed Leveridge, "we have struck a Massachusetts regiment. There is Barnard, and Oakland, and the rest. Halloa, Oakland, how are you?" he shouted.

"Why, Horton's here!" broke out Dalton, who

had recognized his friend. "How did he get over to this wing of the army?"

In a few moments the two officers had dismounted, and were shaking hands, embracing, and exhibiting such demonstrations of hearty friendship as would seem absurd any where out of the army.

"What sort of a place is this?" asked Leveridge. "Here, for five hours, we have been hunting up a road for our corps to march over, but haven't found so much as a tow-path."

"March over!" cried Oakland. "Why, colonel, we've been swimming. Look at these soldiers; look at us. Tell me the color of my trowsers, if you can. We've been swimming, I tell you, just four miles, and this is the first dry land we have seen, and isn't it a Paradise?"

"The semi-nude condition of some of these black people is about the only suggestion of the Garden of Eden that I can see," said Leveridge, as, looking around, he worked a passage-way through his thick mustache to make way for a cup which had been handed him, containing a liquid substance strongly resembling water.

Meanwhile Dalton and Horton were reciting to each other their varied experiences since the two wings of the army had separated at Savannah.

G

"Not hearing any thing of the advance of the left wing for several days, the general has sent me across country to find it. I had but just dismounted when you came in sight. I shall halt here for an hour or two to feed and rest the horses," said Horton. "Our columns have been concentrated at Pocotaligo for the last two days, although we have not been idle. General Howard is with the Seventeenth Corps, which forms our right, and is trying to force the passage of the Salkahatchie at Beaufort's Bridge. After I left head-quarters yesterday morning I took a southwest course. About ten miles out we ran into a squad of rebel cavalry, but managed to get through with only one man hurt, and he not seriously. Do you know where we are, Colonel Barnard?"

"Not precisely," answered that officer. "Since we came upon this place we have been trying to get the brigade into camp. These flat lands, so sparsely inhabited, are about as blind a country to march through as I ever saw, but I am sure we are marching in a northwest direction, and that Loper's Crossroads, Allandale, Fiddler's Pond, etc., are somewhere ahead of us. Perhaps that negro can give us information. Halloa, there, Sam, Bill, Cæsar, Jack, George Washington, come here; I wish to speak with you."

The man thus addressed was black as a coal, without any trace of white blood in color or feature. He gazed vacantly at the group of officers. He seemed to know that he was addressed, but understood not a word.

"Come here! Are you deaf?" again cried the colonel. The poor fellow did not move.

"Bob!" shouted Oakland to a young negro servant who had joined the regiment near Milledgeville, and who was seated upon a camp-chest busily employed in stripping a chicken. As he came shambling up to the party, there was on his face a grin of ecstatic delight for which there was no especial occasion. "I wish you to talk to that black man. Stop your grinning."

"Yaas, cap'n," and Bob broke in a fearful "Ki-yi," which was intended for a laugh. At the same time he slapped his legs with his soldier's cap, which was ornamented with the chicken's wing-feathers.

"Ask him," said Oakland, "to whom this plantation belongs, what is his own name, and where this road leads to."

"Yaas, cap'n," ejaculated Bob, and he appealed to the black man in a pompous manner, which he intended should inspire him with some idea of the importance of the occasion.

"Look a heyar, sah. Wha yer no speak ter de

cap'n? He's one ob Massa Sherman's company, dat he is. Who's yer massa? Wha yer stan dere starin' like a turkey-gobbler? Wha don yer talk right out?"

The plantation slave gazed into Bob's face as if he sought for some words familiar to his ear. He muttered some strange gibberish, and then sank back into an expression of utter stupidity.

"Cap'n," said Bob, desperately, "he wus nor a down-South nigger. He's no shuck, sah, nohow."

"We will try him in some other language," said Oakland. "You may clear out, Bob."

"Est ce que vous parlez Français?"

The negro's face was as blank as an Egyptian statue, which he resembled not a little.

"Sprechen sie Deutsch?" cried Leveridge, with a broad, thick accent, which would have done credit to a month's residence in the Bowery.

Evidently the man had never tasted lager bier, nor sunned himself beneath the walls of Göttingen University.

"Parlati Italiano?" asked another. But the negro was ignorant of the land of Petrarch and Michael Angelo.

"Hablato Española?" resumed Oakland.

At the musical sounds of the Spanish tongue the

"We can't make any thing out of the poor fellow," said Colonel Barnard.

poor slave's eyes brightened for a moment. He uttered some unmeaning sounds, hesitated, and ceased speaking.

"We can't make any thing out of the poor fellow," said Colonel Barnard. "I wonder who and what he is. He certainly is neither deaf nor dumb."

"If you were to live in the South many years, you would find some strange characters upon these plantations," remarked Dalton. "This man is evidently a recent importation from Africa, and speaks only his native tongue. You observed in him signs of intelligence when he heard the sounds of the Spanish language, which were most likely an echo of his life in the Spanish barracoons, where these people are often kept for weeks before the traders can get them on board the slave-ships."

"Do you imagine that slaves from the African coast have been brought into the South during the war?" demanded Horton, with an expression of surprise and indignation.

"Certainly," was Dalton's response; "I am sure of it; and more than that, before the war, cargo after cargo of these wretched creatures were landed here. What was there to prevent a slave-ship from running up the Broad, the Ogeechee, or the Altamaha rivers, and landing a cargo of human beings, whose bodies and souls cost but a few trinkets in Africa, but who were worth from five hundred to a thousand dollars a head on these bottom-lands? This negro, I should suppose, was from the south of Africa; but you will find upon the plantations a hundred different types and tribes from all parts of Africa. Near Darwin, in Georgia, before the war, I could have shown you a Foulah negro, who was born and lived in the country of Soudan, in the north of Africa. He is a strict Mohammedan, has his Koran in the Arabic, and reads it daily. He abstains from spirituous liquors, and keeps all the fasts, particularly those of the Ramadan. What has become of this man during the war it would be a curious thing to know, for he was a most uncommon character."

"He is an exception, then, to the large majority of these unfortunate people," interposed Leveridge. "I have had occasion to travel over hundreds of these plantations during our campaigns, and ninety-nine out of one hundred of the field-hands are more senseless than I ever believed human beings could be."

"That is a melancholy truth," said Horton, "and whether or not we conquer the South, what a future of woe have these poor creatures!"

"That and the future rehabilitation of the South

are two questions which fill me with forebodings," answered Dalton.

"For my part," said Horton, "I am full of hope. It will require generations to educate these blacks out of their degradation; and as for their former masters, I believe the horrible enormity of the vice of mastership was the poisoned virus which incited to this treasonable crusade against our government. But, with freedom to the blacks, I have faith that there will come about a gradual but a complete reorganization of society on principles of morality, justice, and patriotism."

"I agree with you, Horton," said Barnard. "By George! we have known to our bitter cost that these Southerners are brave, and have given up their property and their lives for what they believe to be the truth. Yes, gentlemen, they have a foundation of manliness which will bear good fruit one of these days."

"I can not forget Andersonville, Salisbury, Libby, and Belle Isle," answered Dalton, with emphasis. "My personal wrongs I may be able to put aside, but the atrocities committed upon our prisoners will never pass from my memory."

"Let us make a distinction, Dalton, between the authors of these crimes and thousands of people who have been either forced into the war or have been deluded," said Horton.

"It's hard to make distinctions where a nation (and the South has people enough to make up half a dozen German Principalities) is as large as the South. Now—"

Leveridge suddenly halted in what he had evidently intended should be a long dissertation. For a full half hour his eyes had wandered in the direction of the jubilant Bob. Following the movements of that individual with an eager, mysterious curiosity, his ear now caught the tinkling sound of a bell. He dropped most unceremoniously the subject of reconstruction, and asked,

"Why does that bell ring?"

"It is the method sometimes adopted in certain semi-civilized portions of the globe for announcing dinner," answered Oakland, with gravity.

The party of hungry officers did not wait for farther explanation, but moved with becoming speed toward the big wooden shutter which had been suddenly converted into a dinner-table.

"What is the meaning of this?" asked Leveridge, as he gazed upon a white linen table-cloth which covered the rough board. "Absolutely a tablecloth, white and clean! My duty as inspector requires me to make a note of this. Ah!" he continued, as he made furious assault upon the chicken, potatoes, rice, and other luxuries which loaded his plate, "the army is fast becoming demoralized when its soldiers eat off from linen, and pure linen at that!"

"We could explain, colonel," answered Oakland, who before the war had never known severer hardship than that which a nervous sensibility experiences from a Boston east wind; "but does not Balzac say that 'digestion, in employing human forces, excites an interior sensation that, with gourmands, is equivalent to the enjoyment of love? Many a suicide has been averted at the edge of death by the remembrance of a good dinner.' Let us eat, then, and be happy."

If a stranger to army life had broken in upon this party of light-hearted, jovial men eating their roughly-prepared meal, or if his eye had wandered across the inclosure to the line of shelter-tents, where groups of soldiers could be seen laughing, or singing and dancing to the music of a violin, he would scarcely believe that these men had all day waded through mud and water, driving before them the enemy's cavalry, or that they imagined that the morrow was to bring another day of just such painful toil, or perhaps of battle and death. No. They were as happy as brave men may be — as happy as if the past had no remembered hardship, or the future no apprehended danger.

XXIII.

IT was fortunate for Dalton and Horton that the cavalry corps of the army, under Kilpatrick, was moving forward the morning after the rencontre of these two soldier friends. War does not stifle and extinguish the finer sensibilities of the soldier, so that he does not shrink from traveling in the track of an invading army. He sees and sympathizes with his comrades pierced and torn by shot and shell, but this suffering, which is reflex — for it may any moment become his own case — is displaced by the excitement of the hour, by the drums beating, the shrill bugle-calls, the roar of cannon and rattle of musketry, the whirl and eddy of the fight, the sight of gleaming bayonets, the wild charge, and the exultant cheers of the victors. Your loved friend falls at your side,

"Are you hurt badly?"

With a smile upon his white lips, he answers,

"I think not; don't wait for me. That shout comes from our boys; they are carrying the left of the line. Go ahead! tell me all about it afterward."

You see him carried to the rear; you press on with the victorious host, and for the moment he is forgotten. He came there and took his chance. He is wounded. He may die. But he scorns pity, and calmly reads his fate in the surgeon's eyes. Your turn may come next, and you can not waste the hour in useless lament. You accept whatever may be thrown up for you in this game of war—a bullet or a brevet. The field after a battle has its horrors, but the dead sleep peacefully there, and the memory of their heroism is inspiring. The poor body may lie in the swamp or under the hill-side, but the soul which fought the battle still fights on elsewhere in some other sphere.

But oh! the woe, the utter desolation which follows in the footsteps of an invading foe! Fields wasted, fences destroyed, granaries swept clean of corn, crops trampled out of life, cattle of all kinds, and every vegetable which may be used or eaten, all swept into the ravenous maw of the marching monster! The traveler upon the far Western prairie, away beyond the outposts of civilization, sees even in the wild desert which surrounds him the promise of glorious things. But here, where the man in arms treads, the fruit is blasted, the stalk withered. Your heart aches at the wanton waste. You ride swiftly by through deserted villages. You are deaf—for you must be—to the cries of fainting mothers covering their starved dead children among the ashes of homes once so happy! You must press on with pitiless haste, and shut out from eye, and ear, and heart these despairing moans of helpless ones—these visions of death. Happy will you be if you can forget them also.

As between treason and a vindication of the dignity of the law, the account was more than balanced in these early winter days of 1865.

Our two soldier friends were glad to take some other way to their commands. The second day of their journey brought the column far northward of what was likely to be the head of column to the right wing, and the two officers concluded at once to strike across the country in its search.

XXIV.

THE party was strengthened by a company of tried veterans, under command of a Captain Esting, and, as they rode away upon a side road, leading in a direction at right angles to the course they had been pursuing, they passed into a more thickly settled district. The black stalks of last year's cotton was standing in the fields. Large stacks of corn-fodder were piled up here and there. The fences were in good order, and about the barns, outhouses, and dwellings of the planters there was an air of negligence—that inevitable attendant upon unpaid labor—yet there were many indications of wealth and respectability. The white inhabitants were all of the female sex. Now and then there was a decrepit old man seen in his arm-chair upon the piazza, or some half-witted boy, who stared vacantly at the troop of horsemen as they moved by, but no able-bodied men were to be found, except the negroes, who, of all ages and both sexes, flocked from their work and their cabins to the roadside to see, as they termed them, "dese strange people."

Little halt did our party of soldiers make except to ask some question as to the direction of the road, or if there were any of the enemy near. But they were marching out of the main routes of travel, and the inhabitants could not, or would not, give them any satisfactory information.

"It is about an hour before sunset, and I think we have come twenty miles since we left Kilpatrick," said Horton.

"Yes," replied his friend, "we have come fully that distance, and it is about time we saw something of our foraging parties; they usually spread out fifteen or twenty miles from the main column."

"Unless the rebels are pretty thick at the front," remarked Captain Esting; "and I think we have found one or the other of these now, for I see the advanced guard has halted in the road. I'll soon find out," and he gave his horse the spur and dashed forward down the road.

"Our men are firing!" cried Dalton.

"And they're coming back," said Horton. "Close up well, and move forward at a trot!" he shouted to the officer in command of the detachment of troopers.

They soon met the advanced guard, now retreating, and firing rapidly as they fell back. Gaining the brow of a slight elevation, Horton came in sight of a squadron of the enemy's cavalry a few hundred yards ahead in the road. They were somewhat confused by the deadly fire from the repeating rifles of the Union soldiers, but were evidently preparing to make a charge. Farther on, and to the left of the road, was a large house in the centre of an open field; about the house and in the field were parties of horsemen hurrying hither and thither, some trying to catch their animals, others saddling, and all in commotion at what must have been to them an unexpected approach of the Yankees.

At a glance Horton saw that his little party were more than twice outnumbered.

"We have the advantage of position, and are prepared for a fight. Our salvation is in pitching in," he said, as his quick eye took in the whole situation.

"That's my idea precisely—and with the sabre," answered Esting.

Dalton said nothing, but, with his usual determination, had already drawn his sword, and was loosening his pistols in the saddle holsters. The woods on either side of the road where they stood were open, and admirably selected for the bold attack contemplated by Horton. In twenty seconds the band of less than one hundred brave men were formed in double line, with an interval of twenty feet between.

"Draw sabres!" shouted the captain; "charge!" and away they thundered down the hill with a loud hurrah.

The enemy heard the cry and saw the swiftly-advancing line. Huddled together in the road, the leading platoon of Confederates was broken and disordered by the crowd pressing from behind. A few dashed bravely forward to meet the onset of the Yankees, led by Horton, Dalton, and Esting, but the shock was irresistible. In the road, in the ditch, to the right and left, down went the enemy, horse and rider. The gallant hundred swept around on either flank of the bewildered foe, to whom they appeared a thousand. There was a wild hurly-burly; the sabres rose and fell. "For God and the Union!" was the cry. In vain did the confused enemy answer with the revolver; their shots flew wild; and still the sabres leaped and crashed, their bloody blades crimson in the luird light of the sun. It was a short, sharp struggle, and then the blinded, staggering mass of men broke and fled in dismay.

"Follow them a while, Esting, until you get them into a good run. Give them the Spencers now, but don't go too far," said Horton, who watched the pursuing party for a moment, and then rode up to where Major Dalton had dismounted from his horse.

"Have we lost many men?" asked the major, who was reloading his pistols.

"There is one poor fellow killed, and several slightly hurt. But what's the matter with you? There is the blood running out of your sleeve."

"It's nothing but a slight cut. I have used the arm since. There were two of these fellows dashed at me at the same moment. One of them was Ghilson, an old Savannah acquaintance, who had a personal spite against me. This is the first time we have met during the war. We recognized each other at once, and, unless I am mistaken, he will not forget the meeting, for I answered his cut with a thrust full in quart which badly-gashed his face." And so Dalton had answered Ghilson's challenge of four years ago.

XXV.

THE wounded men were at once removed to the house already spoken of. It proved to be superior in every way to the buildings of this class usually found upon plantations. It now seemed almost deserted by all but the negroes, who welcomed the new-comers with ecstatic exclamations of joy.

"Well, what now, Baxter?" asked Horton, as his orderly came hastily forward to meet him, with an expression of satisfaction mingled with a shadow of dismay.

"I have found that colored man Zimri, sir."

"The man who killed the rebel spy in the mountains?"

"Yes, captain; but he's in a heap of sorrow now. It 'pears like as if this was the plantation he was fetched up on. His mother lives here. When that scrimmage began, she ran to see after Zimri, and a stray shot hit her, and I think she's gone up. They're in the first cabin on the right, there."

The negro quarters were, as usual, coarsely built of logs. It was easy for Horton to distinguish the cabin of Zimri's mother from the rest, for about the door, peering into the windows and into the cracks between the logs, was a crowd of negroes, most of them about the middle age. The calamity which had fallen upon Aunt Fannie overcame every feeling of curiosity common usually to these people.

"De Lord hab mercy on her soul!" murmured an old negress, whose wrinkled and haggard face and blinking eyelids told the story of her extreme age. Resting her jaws upon the palms of her hands, she stared into vacancy, muttering to herself,

"Yah, yah, de Lord teks car his own, an' Fannie is de Lord's own chile. More dan fifty years sin I tuk her fro' her mudder's arms. She was a angel den, an' she's bin a angel ebber sin. Yaas," she cried, in a shrill and broken voice, while she stretched forth her hands, whose bent and bony fingers trembled with the palsy of age. "Yaas, de Lord be praised, dere is rest fur de weary. I see de mansions ob bliss openin'· ter receibe her. She'll war a robe ob white, an' she's gwine whar ther'll be no sorrer nor sighin' any more."

The old woman's face, as these words came forth with the impress of prophecy, was filled with a wild, exultant look, as if, standing upon the verge of eternity, she saw visions of the spirit-world. For the instant her utterances hushed the groans and cries of her companions, who gazed upon her with superstitious fear, while a sense of awe took possession of even the two officers.

"Clar de way!" "Move yer hoofs, Dinah!" "Don yer see der ossifers want to go in dar!" were the exclamations from one to another, as Horton and Dalton moved among the crowd toward the door. A strange, pathetic spectacle met their gaze. The light of the setting sun streamed through the open doorway full upon the figure of a woman stretched upon a low cot in the farther corner of the room. Facing them, and kneeling upon the floor, was a gray-haired negro, whose raised hands were clasped in the attitude of prayer. Upon the edge of the bed sat Zimri. His face was turned toward the suffering, dying mother, while he held both her hands in his. In the broad fireplace lay a few brands smouldering in the white ashes. The walls and ceilings were begrimed with smoke. Horton, who had been studying every detail of this picture of human woe, was suddenly aroused by the voice of the dying woman. The words came faint and broken from her lips; the red blood bubbling from her wound as each breath came and went. She was not conscious of what she said, for, could she have looked into the face of her son, which was by turns black with passion and then stricken with grief, she would have died and left the tale untold.

"Massa Ralph! Massa Ralph! don't you speak such dreadful words. Charlotte is Zimri's wife. Charlotte, my chile, you mus' not go dar; 'tis sinful afore God. Come to me. Dar! close to my heart. He dare not touch his ole nurse. Dar, right dar!" whispered the dying, raving woman. For a moment no sound escaped her lips, when, with a bound, she sprang up, stretching out her trembling arms, screaming in frantic grief, "Ralph! Massa Ralph! for de love ob Christ, do not take her away. Charlotte! Charlotte! you're my son's wife. Why go away with that wicked man. Zimri! Zimri! my son, your wife, Charlotte—"

With a cry of anguish Zimri clasped his mother in his arms, while great sobs shook his strong frame.

"Oh, mother, it is Zimri who speaks to you—who holds you here. Look at me. Speak to me. Do you not know me? Say but a word!"

For a brief instant the delirium passed from her eyes, and with it came recognition—a sickly smile. She tried to speak, but the words would not come.

Her bosom ceased to throb, and her arms slowly unwound themselves from about Zimri's neck; her head fell back, her eyes were fixed, and she was dead.

Zimri buried his head in his hands, and nursed his double grief.

"This is terrible," said Dalton; "that man will break his heart."

"I know him well; his is a nature that will not bend," answered Horton, "and he will die if he is not distracted from this sorrow."

The old negro, who had risen from his knees, came forward.

"You is right, genl'men, Zimri is a powerful strong mind, but dere is relief in prayer. It is ter de Lord he mus' look for help in time o' trouble." Stepping to the door, he spoke to the crowd of negroes, who did not fully understand the cause of the silence within. Lifting up his hands, while his patriarchal face glowed with benign expression, he said,*

---

* It has been said that the exhibition by the negroes of intense feeling on religious subjects was an expression of one form of obedience to their masters. While I have no doubt but what the superstitions of the blacks was an element always fostered and directed for the mental as well as physical enslavement of these people, yet the master "builded better than he knew," for the children of the slaves are taught by their parents to pray and sing as soon as they can talk, and from that time there never comes a moment when they do not go to God with all their grief and woes, and with a sub-

"Brederen and sisters, de Lord is in dis house. He has come down and taken Fannie. Dere, hush now; do not weep, nor cry out, for sister Fannie is gone whar dere is no weepin' nor sorrow. Her name is written in de Lamb's book ob life. Let us pray dat, wid sister Fannie, we may stan' wid de white robes afore de great white trone."

Then the old preacher knelt down, lifting up his face in the fading twilight, and poured forth his soul in fervent prayer to that God of infinite love and pity who comes very near to his weak and suffering children. In the presence of death there is no distinction of rank or race, and Dalton and Horton reverently bowed their heads before the sublime pathos of that simple-hearted old man as he prayed—

"O Lord Almighty! dy chast'ning han' is come right down here an' took away sister Fannie. Dar is her poor bleedin' body, but de soul is gone far away among de angels, whar dere is chantin' an' singin' forebber an' ebber afore de great white trone.

---

lime faith that he is no "respecter of persons." The simple tenets of the Methodist Church have brought the Christian religion within the comprehension of the most ignorant of these people; and whatever may have been the apostasy of the churches of whites in the South during the rebellion, certain it is that the religion of Christ was kept pure in the hovels of the despised slaves.

De Lord Jesus knows his flock, an' sister Fannie is dar in de mansions ob de blessed angels. O Lord Jesus, sanctify us by dis dispensation. Come berry near us, right ter our hearts, so dat when de angels come fur us we shall be ready widout a complaint. Dar is Zimri, he's bin a good son ter his mudder. Gib him, O Lord, de peace of Christ. Make his heart clean, so dat he'll join her above, whar we all shall sing an' praise de Lord forebber and ebber. Amen."

Before the preacher had finished this simple petition, the men and women were weeping and crying out, "Yes, Lord!" "We's waitin' fur de comin' ob Christ!" "Hallelujah!" and other fervent exclamations. As the "Amen" left the old man's lips, with one accord they broke forth into a sad chant, sung in that mournful minor key which seems to have grown out of their life of hopeless servitude.* A

---

* While the negroes in their songs are not governed by any strict rules of metre, they always manage, no matter how many words they may crowd into a line, to keep perfect time. In the life of freedom which opens before the blacks of the South, these sad songs, which have expressed to me more than any other feeling an utter sense of hopelessness on this side of the grave, will be lost. Both the words and the peculiar music belong to the slave-life, and it will surely give place to a more cheerful music, and more significant of the joyous, contented characteristics of the negro nature. Will not some competent hand record these singular melodies for the benefit of history?

single voice first took up the song, but old and young joined in the refrain in full chorus:

"Dere's room enough in heaben, for all de angels say
    Dere's room enough.
My God says dere's room enough,
    Sinner, don't stay away—
    Don't stay away.
My Lord says dere's room enough—
    Don't stay away."

"Way ober in de Promised Land, in de Promised Land,
    In de Promised Land.
My Lord calls forth, and I mus' go to meet him
    In de Promised Land,
    In de Promised Land.
My chil'n in de Promised Land; my mudder in de Promised Land,
    In de Promised Land."

Hardly had the chorus of this psalm died away when another voice broke forth in a shorter, more cheerful metre—

"Gwine on de island, oh dica—
Gwine on de island, oh dica—
Gwine on de island, way on de odder shore.
Oh, gwine dica—
Oh, gwine dica—
Oh, gwine dica, way on de odder shore."

By this time the crowd of negroes had reached a pitch of excitement which it is impossible to describe, and which can not be understood except by those who have witnessed these singular exaltations.

The singing was interspersed by shouts of "Hallelujah!" "Glory!" "Glory to God!" The women seemed the most impressed, some springing into the air, others twisting about upon the ground; both women and men were rocking their bodies and swaying about. All at once they broke forth in one voice—

> "Jubilate! jubilate!
> The world calls me Swonga.
> O Lord! Swonga;
> What makes you tink of Swonga.
> For my Lord Jesus, whar you tink I foun' him—
> Down in de lonesome valley.
> How you tink I foun' him; I work my knee-bone bending
> Way down in de lonesome valley.
> Jubilate! jubilate!"

The plaintive melody ended as suddenly as it began, and then Horton advanced to the bedside, and placed his hand upon Zimri's shoulder,

"Zimri, my friend."

The son of the slave woman turned his head at the kind words so gently uttered, and recognized Captain Horton.

"I did not think to meet you again so soon, and in this way. Oh, sir, she was all that was left me on earth, except—" and his voice faltered—"Charlotte. My poor, loving mother!" and he turned once more toward the humble cot.

"Zimri, you must leave her for the present. This

terrible misfortune has been caused by our presence here. But for this fight she would have been alive and well. In a degree I feel responsible for the disaster."

"It is not for you to censure yourself. God has chosen his own time and way. Perhaps she had better not have lived longer. But it seems as if I had lost my last and only friend."

Horton led Zimri away from the cabin, while Dalton, who had witnessed this sad tragedy with a heart of sympathy, remained to give directions for the burial of the body.

"We came here only this morning," said Zimri, in reply to Horton's queries. "After I left you in the mountains of Alabama, I found General Ralph. I had but a few words with my wife Charlotte when the general sent me away with Major Ghilson. I have not seen either Charlotte or the general since. I have tried to find Charlotte, but the commands have been widely separated. I learn that both of them were here a few days ago. The dying words of my mother fill me with alarm."

"Zimri, you must take my friendly advice, and give up this pursuit. I am sure nothing good will come of it."

"Captain Horton, you are kinder to me than I deserve, but I can not give up Charlotte to the power of that devil. I shall follow them as soon as my poor mother is in her grave."

Horton no longer attempted to dissuade Zimri from his purpose. There was a vindictive glare in the man's eye, and a firm setting of the lips, which proclaimed his determination to satisfy his doubts.

It was a weird sight Fannie's burial. It was at night, and the pitch-pine torches flaming in the wind threw a sombre light upon the group of negroes gathered about the grave.

The old preacher uttered a few words over the coffin now lowered into the grave. The earth soon covered it from view, and then, amid the prayers and blessings of the negroes who flocked around him, Zimri, with the officers, mounted their horses and filed down the avenue out into the road.

Before the morning sun had risen, the party of Union soldiers had reached the head-quarters of their army, and Zimri, within the rebel lines, held Charlotte trembling in his arms.

XXVI.

HIS brother, General Ralph Buford, was not at the head-quarters of his brigade when Zimri arrived there. He had been called suddenly to Branchville to consult with Beauregard and other Confederate officers. Sherman's troops appeared at so many places at the same moment that his real movement was undefined. Meanwhile his troops had been thrown across the line of the railroad, and then across the Edisto River, and General Buford was cut off from his command.

Three days of happy forgetfulness were these to Zimri. Saddened and subdued by his mother's death, he was only too content to rest in the love of Charlotte, gazing into her golden-brown eyes, and listening to her words of tenderness. Zimri was not suspicious by nature. His affection for his wife was the ruling, absorbing passion of his life; and when she met him with a cry of gladness, and wound her arms

ZIMRI AND CHARLOTTE.

about his neck, and murmured her welcome into his willing ear so lovingly, all past suffering and agonizing doubt fled both from thought and memory.

It was the day of the capture of Columbia that they sat together upon the bank of the Congaree, near the city. They were heedless of the stir and alarm which agitated the citizens. They regarded not the messengers dashing to and fro on errands of hate and fear. The boom of the distant cannon did not disturb their happy dream.

Charlotte was little changed from the beautiful daughter of the sun whom we saw among the mountains of Alabama a few months ago. Exposure to the open air had tinged her cheek with a richer color, but the same dark tresses waved gracefully away from her fair forehead. Her eyes had not lost their liquid purity; her form had the same charming languor in repose as of old, and the same beautiful grace in motion.

"After to-morrow, Charlotte, we shall get away from this fettered life. Within the Union lines we shall find freedom and friends, and such a home as the slave never knows here. I have a debt of gratitude to pay Mrs. Buford, who is at Winnsboro', and may need assistance. We will go there, and then take the first chance of escape."

"Let us not wait till to-morrow," pleaded his wife, as she drew closer to him. "Oh, Zimri, every moment we stay here is dangerous. Master Ralph may return any moment, and then—" Her golden eyes were veiled by their long lashes, and she hesitated.

"I know what you would say, my darling: 'General Ralph will not let us remain together.' But he shall not separate us again—he dare not! I would be glad never to meet him, but he can't protect Mrs. Buford after the Confederate army has passed her, and I can. We must not forget, Charlotte, that there are years of kind words and deeds which we both owe to her. Has she not taught you to read and to write, adding knowledge to the graces of my beautiful Charlotte?" and Zimri kissed her with fondness.

"Dear Zimri, I am not ungrateful—indeed I am not—but I am afraid. I don't dare think of going there."

"You need not be afraid," said Zimri, in a tone which drove the color from his wife's cheek. "If it comes to the worst, I can protect you too; if not by an appeal to reason, there is still a last resort left, even for slaves."

When the husband and wife returned to headquarters they found the camp in commotion. Buford had returned, but at imminent risk of his life.

His small party had been attacked, and all but himself and two men had either been killed or captured. In addition to this, it was ascertained that the enemy had crossed the river above Columbia, and were marching rapidly upon the city.

When the general's eyes fell upon Zimri, there passed over his face an expression of hate which might seem to have been borrowed from the under world. Zimri looked into his brother's face unflinchingly. Each was ready to give expression to the emotions which swayed him, but it was no time now for the encounter. There were other things which could not be postponed that imperatively called Buford's attention in another direction. There was a large army sweeping around him, and escape was only possible on the instant. As the general moved away, Zimri plunged into the woods, following the direction taken by the wagons an hour before.

XXVII.

A MOST unfortunate incident connected with the capture of Columbia was the terrible conflagration occasioned by the reckless conduct of the defenders in setting fire to the thousand bales of cotton which had been placed in the streets for that purpose. It was a sad sight to see that morning, after the fire, thousands of women and children, deprived of food and shelter, wandering among the ruins of once happy homes. There was fear and despair in the hearts of these people, who had reviled the government of their fathers, who had cursed with the bitterness of hate these Northerners, conquerors now.

This was a mournful spectacle; but on this same memorable morning Columbia presented a sight which more than compensated for this dark picture of suffering, although it also suggested many painful thoughts by way of retrospect. It was the vision of five hundred rescued prisoners, whose eyes had grown feeble staring at blank prison walls, but were now restored to strength at sight of the old flag, the symbol to them of freedom and home. With prayerful, unspeakable joy, they fell upon their knees and wept. Oh! you who have ever had the freedom of the open air, you can not comprehend the joy of release from a rebel prison. The victims who survived this prison-life shrink from its memories. No tongue may describe its horrors, and only in "Fidelio," that masterpiece of Beethoven, has it found expression even in the mournful strains of music.

Among the crowd of escaped prisoners that thronged the quarters of the commanding general there came, under the charge of the guard, a wretched, sickly-looking man, with lack-lustre eyes, shoeless and ragged. He had that day come within the Union lines, and had been arrested as one of the rebel army. He had a pitiful tale to tell—the old story of conscription and of despotic infliction of suffering. It was a common story, but his whole appearance testified to its truthfulness. This man was received cautiously, but was kindly treated. If those who had been confined in rebel prisons had reason to rejoice over their release, certainly he had equal reason, for he had that day escaped not only from a forced service, but from persecution that knew no pity, and had no cause but a relentless hate.

XXVIII.

AS Zimri pressed on in the effort to find General Buford's head-quarters train, he found the woods, the roads, and the by-ways filled with flying men. These, in their panic of fear, in their eagerness to rush out of sight and sound of the death-dealing guns of the enemy, threw away their arms, and even their clothing. They lost all sense of place and direction. Many fled into the Union lines unawares; others dropped fainting with terror and exhaustion upon the roadside, in the swamp, and in the forest. It was a confused mass of men, material, and animals impelled by an instinct of flight northward. The winter wind, cold and cheerless, added to their misery, and during their temporary halts, as they surrounded their dreary camp-fires, they elbowed aside their commanding officers, and seemed regardless of all military discipline and the usual proprieties of the service:

The place where Buford's men halted for the night was a ruined plantation. Broken, half-burned fences, tall chimneys blackened with smoke, a heap of brick, with here and there a window-cap or door-sill, told where a house had stood in happier times. A few negro huts could be seen crowded with women and children.

Zimri had succeeded in his search. Himself unrecognized, he now became witness to a most pitiful, agonizing scene. From his concealment he saw General Buford approach a building used for the storage of cotton, which he had appropriated for the night. He saw him turn to the group near by before he entered, and, after a brusque "Good-night," call for Charlotte. He saw her hesitate, and then, at Buford's second and more impatient call, he saw her move in obedience to his command. He heard the group left behind utter their jests, careless and coarse, occasioned by this circumstance.

He was on fire with rage. Madly he wandered through the woods during the cheerless night, heeding not the biting blasts of the north wind. He cried out savagely for revenge—cried out against this cowardly brother, against his treacherous wife. The white pines looked sadly down upon him, but gave no answer to his moans.

Midnight found him back again at the camp-fire where lay the sleeping group, unconscious of his presence — back again in the neighborhood of a dreadful reality, nameless and inexplicable.

The gray morning at length breaks upon a dismal sight. There is just light enough to see the yard, deserted by the band encamped there last night. One by one, with that supreme selfishness which in a panic makes every man clutch at the remotest chance offered him for life, they have all stolen away. In the distance is heard the sullen boom of the enemy's artillery, indicating a relentless pursuit. A horseman dashes wildly by. He looks neither to the right nor to the left, riding onward, onward, thinking only of flight; and then all is desolate and still, as if the Angel of Death hovered about the place.

Suddenly there shoots up into the leaden sky a bright light, which reveals a terrible disaster. In an instant the log house in which Buford has made his quarters is one sheet of roaring flame. The unpacked cotton, the pitch-pine logs burn with a rapidity rivaling the explosion of powder. A column of black smoke rises above a furnace of living fire. Screams of agony, smothered cries of pain, rage, and despair, pierce through the flames. There is no help,

"And Zimri, leaning against the trunk of a withered pine by the roadside, looks on."

no hope—there is a crash of falling timbers—there rises and flies as high as heaven an ink-black cloud of smoke and whirling brands, and then there is a lull—a dreadful silence. And Zimri, leaning against the trunk of a withered pine by the roadside, looks on. His arms are folded, and his face wears an expression of vindictiveness and of triumph. He looks like the incarnation of awful retribution and revenge; and the victims—these are Charlotte and—

But why does Zimri spring into the road with the cry and bound of an angry tiger robbed of his prey? In the dim, shadowy border of the wood he sees the figure of a man on horseback steal swiftly away from the smouldering ruins. The steed has neither bridle nor saddle; its rider is clothed in white, his long black hair floating backward in the wind. The pale face of the horseman is turned for a moment toward Zimri, glaring with hate and convulsed with fear. His arm is raised with a wild and threatening gesture, and the vision disappears.

XXIX.

It was one of those bright and beautiful mornings which come in South Carolina in January, when Nature, rising from its brief rest, puts forth a first effort of conscious power. The sun penetrated the mists and clouds, and shone out in semi-tropical splendor. The birds flocked in troops, and, flitting through the air, or gathering in the foliage, warbled and sung in joyous harmony. All nature was glad, singing with its countless tongues a hymn of happiness, and of a peace which seemed as if it might have been eternal.

But war; terrible, cruel war, was in the land. The Grand Army of the Union had left Columbia behind them, and was marching over the roads, spreading out through the pine forests, stretching across the tilled fields, trampling upon the beautiful gardens, and leaving fire and destruction in its track. In order to distract the attention of the enemy from the true point of attack, and the better to obtain food and forage for man and beast, the army had been divided. The two wings marched upon parallel roads, from ten to fifteen miles apart, with orders to concentrate upon Winnsboro' on the morning of the day in which this chapter opens.

By some of those accidents inseparable from the movements of large bodies of armed men with their cumbrous trains—the destruction of bridges, or imperfect roads—the column in which Horton was marching was delayed beyond the hour of conjunction.

Wearied with the frequent halts, tired of watching the patient mules straining to drag their heavy loads through the swamps and sloughs, surfeited even with the sports of foraging parties in chase of pigs and chickens, Horton, Leveridge, and Dalton started for Winnsboro', confident that they would find the other wing of the army in occupation of the city. As they cantered along the smooth road, they noticed the deserted appearance of the farm-houses. The rumor of the approaching army had preceded them, and the frightened people had fled. As they neared the town, evidences of the close proximity of the other wing appeared. Already had the foraging parties visited the inhabitants. Weeping women screamed to the officers from their doorways, and begged for a guard. The "bummers" had entered their house, and had left, what they left at all, in indescribable confusion.

Two miles from the town they saw a long column of troops marching on a hill-side road, their flags flying, their bayonets gleaming in the sunlight, and now and then, as the light breeze stirred the leaves, they caught the strains of far-off martial music. "A race for the town!" was the cry, and with spur and whip they bounded forward, and a few more moments found them in the centre of the public square of the city.

What splendid confusion! What magnificent order was there in those streets, crowded with officers and men! The column of troops was marching in grand array through the city to the stirring music of several bands. Wagons were backed up to warehouse doors to receive their loads of hay and grain; fine coaches, drawn by motley-dressed negroes fresh from slave-life, were driving through the streets loaded with poultry, hams, and other spoils of war; officers and men were hurrying hither and thither, or standing idly by watching the parade, the crowd, the carnival; and yet others were engaged in extinguishing the flames which were in progress when the troops first entered the town.

As Horton gazed upon this exciting spectacle, he remembered the history of this most ancient, most aristocratic of all the Southern cities. What South Carolinians claim of superiority for South Carolina over her sister states, the people of this ancient burg demanded for Winnsboro' over the claims of all other South Carolinians. The hereditary claims of the house of Hapsburg might be questioned; a parvenue may possibly be admitted into the sacred Quartier St. Germain; a bar sinister might be traced upon the escutcheon of a Russell or Westminster; but to question the natural right of a Winnsburgian to rule over all his fellow-creatures, white and black, was a crime never committed within the memory of man.

By to them a sort of natural consequence, statesmen who had led in the affairs of the nation were born and lived there. The onward car of Progress had never passed through Winnsboro'. The people believed as their fathers did before them—believed in property in man; considered secession not rebellion, but a simple assertion of their rights; they believed, too, in their safety and security from the shocks of war; no serpent concealed in the depths of the jungle felt more secure than they. But one fine morning the people of Winnsboro' awoke and found themselves astonished. It could not be, but it was, and their consternation, despair, fear, and rage may be imagined on this bright morning in the beginning of the year 1865.

The party of Union officers were soon separated from each other—Leveridge to search for a camping-ground for the advancing column, Dalton to give directions for the disposition of a quantity of arms and ammunition found in the town. Horton did not move from the position where he had been watching the hurly-burly of the troops, and the grand array of the column as it marched along. He had fallen into one of his reveries, soliloquizing, as was his habit, upon the chances and mischances of war, when he felt a light touch upon his arm. Looking down, he saw standing by the head of his horse the colored man Zimri. At the first glance Horton saw that some terrible event had happened to this man, in whose history he had become so much interested.

He was not the active scout whose keen eye, firm step, and manly bearing had so deeply impressed the captain during the exciting adventure with the rebel spy, nor yet did he have the chastened but earnest face which he had seen a few days before. In the midst of the stately movement before them, among this crowd of vigorous live men, he seemed like one of those lofty pines in the mighty growth of the savannas which yet rears its head cloudward, but whose trunk has been seared and scarred with a thunderbolt. The light of hope was quenched in his eye; his lips were pale; his cheeks colorless. He did not look Horton full in the face, as was his habit; there was an uncertain movement of the body, such as palsied men have. There seemed to have settled down upon the soul of this man an unutterable, incurable woe. He had that expression which Doré has given to his Wandering Jew. By an inevitable law, the internal combat of the soul had imprinted itself upon his face and form. There was something of the remorse which follows crime when good men have committed crime, but that was overshadowed by an expression of utter hopelessness.

Zimri had seen the expression of horror reflected in Horton's face, and he anticipated his inquiry—

"I can not answer your question here and now, if ever. I have a favor to ask of you. Please go and see Mrs. Buford, the wife of—" Zimri checked himself a moment—" General Ralph. Mrs. Buford was very kind to me and mine in the old days. She is frightened for her personal safety, and wished me to send her a Union officer. She lives in that house yonder, sir," and Zimri pointed to a building which had just been saved from burning by the efforts of the soldiers.

"I will go there at once," replied Horton. "Meanwhile you must accompany Baxter to head-quarters; you are unwell, and must be provided for."

"Thank you, captain," said Zimri. "Indeed, I shall be glad to go any where for rest."

In a few moments Horton found himself in the presence of Mrs. Ralph Buford. To explain how this lady, of a refined and sensitive nature, came to be the wife of General Ralph, would open up a feature in the social life of the South which has never yet had its writer, and which it is not within the province of this story to record. Only so much may be told of her in these pages as will serve to weld a link in the chain of events which are now hurrying rapidly to an end. She is but one of the half-lights in the picture, an unwilling prophet in a weird tragedy.

XXX.

MRS. BUFORD was reared in the midst of opulence rare even among the wealthy "gentry" of the South. From her birth she had never known a want ungratified nor a wish denied. She had passed the later years of girlhood in that world of art which greets the cultivated traveler every where in Europe. In the days before the war she was a frequent visitor and marked favorite in the best society of the North; and when public affairs led her father to sojourn in Washington, she became the centre of a select circle of those who, even in that city of ambitious distinctions and distractions, seek the soothing relief of a refined and spiritual life.

When Horton first saw her, an unwonted excitement had imbued her pale cheek with a delicious rose-tint; her pure gray eyes beamed with unnatural fire; while the course of the blood could be distinctly traced through the veins beneath a skin whose transparency was almost painful to witness.

Horton at once assured her of safety and protection, and he would gladly have ended the interview at that point, for to a soldier of heart and sentiment there can be no experience so painful as to listen to the complaints and angry protestations of those who are the helpless victims of the rigors of war. Like most women of the South when discussing the war, Mrs. Buford would not listen to argument nor reason. With unrestrained impetuosity, she gave free scope to her enthusiasm and her honest but ungovernable impulses.

"You would make us slaves, sir, to your vulgar Northern democracy. You will not succeed in crushing out the spirit of independence of the South Carolinian, although you may trample upon our fields and burn our cities."

"Your house, madam," answered Horton, "was saved from destruction this morning by the efforts of our soldiers, but we will let all that pass. The Union Army proclaims liberty; they do not destroy it. We simply demand allegiance."

"And that we will never own," she replied, and her delicate hands were pressed convulsively to her heart, in the intensity of her emotion, as she continued, "We are fighting for a holy cause; we will struggle and die for it, if need be, and God shall be our judge."

"Your husband is an officer in the rebel army?"

Hesitating slightly, she answered "Yes."

"He is a general in the cavalry corps, is he not?"

"Yes."

"Is this cause which you call 'holy' so sacred that you would be willing to have your husband killed in its defense? Think seriously before you answer."

The blood forsook her face and temples. In her ghastly but beautiful paleness, which was in strong contrast to the masses of dark hair that swept behind her ears in sweet confusion, she seemed like one of those fragile vases that might break by its own exquisite delicacy. Her eyes, which an instant before were gazing into the captain's with intense earnestness, were suddenly introverted as it were, as if searching into the deepest recesses of the heart to find there the absolute truth.

If the human mind were limited in its consciousness and perceptions to the impressions produced by the past, the present, and whatever of the future is within the scope of the external senses, the Realists would be right when they scornfully scout at what is called the supernatural.

The traveler, standing on the Quai d'Ecole, which borders the Seine near the old city of Paris, may witness one of the most picturesque scenes in the Old World. Looking toward the east, the eye is filled with the magnificent proportions of the façade of that grand cathedral, Notre Dame. With what exquisite grace the towers, the columns, the doorways, all in graceful architectural lines, and fretted with curious carvings, the windows gorgeous in harmonious colors, rise before the delighted vision! The eye takes in the exterior of this wonderful work of art, but can not penetrate beyond to the sanctuary within.

But there may be found a photograph of this beautiful scene from the same point of view. By the application of the microscope to the printed photograph, new beauties are revealed to the astonished beholder. He sees through the glass windows, pierces through the gloom which, with endless mysteries, fills and surrounds those solemn arches, and on the opposite wall, beyond the transept, in the chapel of the Holy Virgin, he discovers hanging there a lovely picture of the Immaculate Conception.

What a wonder of mechanical art is this! The sensitive plate in the camera-obscura had accomplished infinitely more than could the power of vision;

and if a mere instrument, "the work of men's hands," powerless without human agency, could achieve so great a marvel, where is the limit of the human spiritual faculty?

We know that in many persons the senses and intellect are educated to heights of perception that sometimes seem almost limitless. Why may they not be quite limitless? and why may not the spiritual nature become so exquisitely sensitive, especially in its correspondence to the souls of others, as to penetrate space itself, and, not cognizant of that which we call time, receive the images of events hidden from the material senses?

Whatever may be the possibilities of man's nature, certain it is that as Horton gazed upon the face of the rebel general's wife, he was chilled with horror, for in a moment it assumed an expression of pain and terror, as if some awful sight had met her gaze. With outstretched hands she moaned,

"Oh no, no, it can not be!".

And then, her mind returning from its wanderings, she saw the Union officer standing there. Pressing her hands to her throbbing temples, then passing them before her eyes as if to remove some scene of terror, she rose to her full height, and, with returning thought, remembered his question. With determined mien and unfaltering voice, she calmly, coldly answered,

"Yes; in the defense of this cause I am willing to see dead the husband whom I love better than life."

As Horton left the wife of General Buford, he wondered not a little at the singular infatuation which had taken possession of the people of the South, and which exhibited itself so painfully in this sensitive and delicate woman. "They believe themselves to be right," he thought. "Will the bitter price they pay for their experience undeceive them? Heaven help them!"

XXXI.

SUPPER was over at the head-quarters camp. In front of the line of fly-tents blazing fires were kindled. The labor of the day was over; the horses and mules, fed and groomed, were lying down to rest. The soldiers who were not on guard were enjoying themselves in many sports—some pitching quoits, others running foot-races or leaping bar. The officers were scattered about. Here a group were studying a map of the country, marking the routes the different corps of the army had already traversed, prognosticating the future of the campaign. Inside of a tent, cross-legged upon his blanket, a knight of sword and spur was earnestly engaged in mending his trowsers or refastening some recusant button. At the end of the line of tents a party were smoking their pipes. Now and then a resonant voice would break forth in song, followed by a chorus which would have startled Maretzek into admiring wonder.

Perhaps the jolliest party of the camp were a group of negroes gathered about a huge barn door, which, placed upon the ground, served as a platform for the dancers.

"Now go way dar wid yer clumsy foot. I'll show yer what de light fantastic toe is," said a big muscular negro as he pushed aside the crowd and stepped upon the platform.

"Who-oo-a, he calls dat hoof a light fantasmam toe," shouted Sam, a Georgia negro, who, since he had joined head-quarters, had exhibited a perpetual grin upon his countenance. On this occasion he roared with laughter. "Yer call dat ar a toe! wha, I tell yer it's all a hoof. Dar is no toe about de premsis."

But the "hoofs" were flying in the air with astonishing rapidity nevertheless, cutting all sorts of capers, performing the neat, intricate, geometrical figures, occasionally descending upon the boards with the force of a trip-hammer.

"Look out dar, Sam; he'll kick dat brack nob clar off yer shoulders," said one.

"De iron-clads do make a noise, sa!" shouted another.

The dancer renewed his *tours de force*. Off went his coat, and still he kicked and twisted; then followed his shirt, revealing the ebony skin covered with perspiration and dust, exhibiting the magnificent muscular proportions of his body and arms, which darted back and forth, and up and down, in frantic gestures. Finally, by a concentrated effort, which seemed to have called into action every muscle and fibre of his body, he sprang into the air, doubling, twisting, and screwing his limbs together, and then, falling upon all-fours, he leaped through the crowd and disappeared amid yells of applause. And then followed another and another sable disciple of Terpsichore, each trying to outdo the other in strength and address, if not in grace, until tattoo was sounded, when they, as well as their white companions, obeyed the call for rest and sleep.

From far and near come these calls. In the camp across the river a drum rolls out its tat, tat, tat; on the hill-side a band pours forth its musical notes; while in the far distance trumpet answers trumpet, until the shivering air, the rocks, and hills, and woods re-echo the sound.

The soldier reading by the camp-fire shuts his book and rolls himself into his blanket; knots of talkers disentangle themselves and separate, each go-

.ing his way; the group of singers chant a last chorus, often of home and loved ones there; the camp-fires lie smouldering, neglected.

In a few brief moments, as if a magic spell had fallen upon the army, a hundred thousand human beings had sank to sleep.

XXXII.

BUT our two friends, Horton and Dalton, are not among the sleeping host. Walking back and forward in the starlight, they are exchanging their confidences: To Horton, Dalton could unfold his story. As it is said that on shipboard men and women reveal more of their true character in a week than in years of social intercourse at home, so it is in the army life. Men stand alone there. The conventionalities which hedge in and control the passions in polite society are stripped away, and men are taken for what they are worth.

Yet in the army, as in society, men have different ways of showing even the good that is in them. Some are what is termed good by the natural indolence of their character; others by calculation; others by vanity. Horton was generous and good because he could not help himself, and thus Dalton poured forth the pent-up emotions of his heart without stint or reservation.

"My dear friend," he said, "I never knew what it was to love in those old days. The noble self-sacrifice of Agnes has aroused in me new and grand sensations, which are strange and solemn. Since we left Savannah, I have begun to learn something of myself. Even out of the regret for what now appears to have been a hopeless suspension of my affection for Agnes, there has risen a firmer faith in myself and a purer devotion to her. In following the grand example she has set me, I have an ambition to reach up to her plane, and stand equal before her."

"Love will accomplish all that and more, Dalton," answered his friend. "I believe most religiously in the power and grace of loving, although in my case I can not say that it has raised me to any great height. The fact is," he continued, in a lugubrious tone, "my love for that dear girl way up there in Boston is a matter of faith. I have no right to suppose that, like Penelope, she sits and sews, waiting for her wandering warrior to return. Yet I seem to have an abiding faith, which makes me think of those knights who went away to the Holy Wars, and came back long years after, gray-bearded and on foot, to find their Evelinas watching from the castle-walls. If I should not see Boston Common for ten years to come, I know I should find Kate still Kate Noble."

"I hope so, from the bottom of my heart," replied his friend. "Who is that in the tent of the general?" he continued, stepping forward.

The canvas cover, toward which the eyes of both were now eagerly directed, like the others on the line, which were the homes of the general's military family, was open from the front, so that the slightest movement of its inmate could be observed from the outside. They could now see that the general had risen from his cot. Thrusting his bare feet into a pair of slippers, he unrolled from a scrap of newspaper a cigar, and then stepped out from such protection as the tent afforded from the falling dew into the open ground. He looked up to the sky, and then out into the darkness, in an absent, half-abstracted way. The night-air was chill, and the camp-fire had burned low. Gathering the ends of the charred rails together, he heaped them upon the still smouldering ashes; then, taking a camp-stool from the tent, he sat down before the fire, which had now kindled into a blaze; he lighted his cigar, and, with his elbows resting upon his knees, gazed earnestly into the bed of coals and flame. The bright light shone full into that iron face, marked with strong lines of thought and care. That bold forehead seemed to project itself higher and broader among the short scrub growth of cross-grained hair. The light caught upon the unbuttoned wristband, taking a warmer glow from the red shirt hardly covering his bare neck.

A strange, grand figure was this sitting there, whose subtle brain at that moment was working out one of the great events in the fate of the nation.

The flame of the fire now gathered new strength, flaring up into the night, revealing the interior of the tent in clearer outline. It was not a gorgeous pavilion, carpeted with velvet and gold, hung with tapestry of silk and wool, furnished with luxurious couch and ease-inviting lounge, with liveried servants to anticipate its owner's slightest wish, surrounded by triple sentinels to guard him from every harm.

There was a singular simplicity—almost a poverty, which marked the head-quarters of the Great Captain.

The tent was a single piece of cotton cloth, stretched from a ridge-pole, where it was held firm to the ground on either side by wooden pegs. A cross-legged camp-cot, a small camp-chest, which is half covered by the uniform thrown carelessly upon it, makes up the scanty furniture. Beside a single candle burnt to its socket there lies a volume of Waverley. A letter-book answers for a writing-table; a valise is the general's only traveling baggage. A number of maps, some opened, and all well worn, lie upon the blanket which answers for a floor to the tent. There was very little pretension about this manège of the commander who had millions at his disposal. This was no Roman consul nor modern emperor traveling in grand state, with pompous mien and brilliant retinue, but a citizen-general of the Republic, not borrowing dignity from adventitious surroundings, but in the simplicity of an unselfish devotion to his country doing the work which lay before him.

There was a weird grandeur, supernaturally picturesque, in this intense stillness, this silent, motionless figure of the chief of thousands of strong men, who slept while he sat watching—the central figure in the grand picture. In the spectral fire-light it seemed almost alone, for the line of tents receded in the darkness on either side. The moon now and then burst through the masses of heavy clouds, revealing groups of tents on the distant hill-side; horses and mules were crouched upon the ground; while behind them rose a forest of pines, filled with mysterious shadows, the graceful tree-tops melting into the veil of blue.

"What a grand subject is that for the pencil of Delaroche or Gerome!" said Horton, who, with his friend, had stood gazing at this picturesque and yet solemn sight. He continued—

"I had rather be able to paint that picture as we see it now than be a general in the regular army."

"It is a remarkable sight," said his friend, "and of peculiar significance."

The two officers resumed their walk. As they passed the general he raised his head.

"Horton," he said, as he recognized him, "I wish you to start off at once upon a reconnoissance. Go to General Howard and ask him for an escort; two companies of mounted infantry will answer. Go back on the road by which we came this morning; about half a mile outside the town you will find a white house, back from the main road a little way."

"I remember it, general."

"By the side of that house, running east, is a road which was used in the Revolutionary War by the English troops, when they had a chain of posts which ran through Camden and Rocky Mount. To-morrow I shall make a right wheel of the army, striking directly for the Santee River. I wish you to push on to the river as quick as you can; ascertain all that may be desirable of the fords and crossings, the condition of the roads, the nature of the bank of the stream, the depth of water, the bed of the stream, and whether it has a rocky or sandy bottom. But you know what I want. The great necessity is speed. Get back as quickly as possible. You will find me with the advance somewhere on the main road to Rocky Mount. By the way, you had better take a good horse. You may need him."

"You may go too, if you like, Major Dalton," continued the general, in answer to that officer's inquiring look.

When Horton, after giving Baxter orders for the saddling of his horse, returned to his tent for his sword and pistols, he found Zimri standing there.

"Ah! Zimri, I thought you had turned in to sleep."

"I don't sleep much of late, captain. Are you going on a scout?"

"Yes."

"Let me go with you, captain. I know every foot of this country—on this and on the other side of the Santee."

"That's just the thing, Zimri, for I do not. Make haste and get your horse, for I will be off in a moment."

XXXIII.

IT was an hour past midnight before the reconnoitring party had turned off from the main road upon the old war-path so clearly designated by the general in his instructions to Horton. Passing the picket-post, they met a foraging party who during the day had lost their way, and were just coming into camp.

"You won't find any Rebs out there, captain. We've been foraging over a right smart piece of country, and didn't come across nary a Reb," was the salutation of the sergeant in charge of the squad of men, laden with chickens, pigs, and other spoils for the cooking mess.

"Thank you," was the response, and the men filed by each other as they moved in opposite directions.

Notwithstanding the assurances of the foragers that there was no enemy near, Horton was too experienced a campaigner and too good a soldier to neglect any precaution in the enemy's country; so he gave orders to the men to preserve strict silence, and the advanced guard were cautioned not to fire, nor give any token of their presence should they come in sight of an enemy, but at once and quietly to fall back. Thus the band of soldiers marched silently along, plunging into the dark woods, splashing across pebbly brooks, emerging into the open country again, but always moving steadily on. Meanwhile Horton called Zimri to his side.

"You told me back at camp that you were acquainted with the country about the Santee River. Why did you suppose I was going there?"

"Because the regions north of this breaks up into steep hills, and an army would find it difficult to cross them with heavy trains. If you march to the east, you will find the country more open, with few hills, and more sandy. You will remember, captain, that it was very nearly upon this route that Greene made his retreat in the old war."

"Yes," replied Horton, "we know that; but I did not understand that this line was chosen so much because of its topographical advantages, but rather as a matter of necessity."

"It was both one and the other," said Dalton.

"And so you think our general has chosen that line, Zimri?"

"Yes, major; if it is not presuming, I did think so."

"Well, Zimri," said Horton, "I hope the rebels are not of the same opinion, as they could give us serious trouble at the river."

The party had now arrived at a point where two roads at an acute angle led into that upon which they were traveling. For a moment there was a halt, while Zimri explained that both roads terminated at the place called Rocky Mount, upon the river's bank.

"I hear horses' hoofs, captain," said Zimri, suddenly.

All the party were silent and listened, but not a breath of sound could be heard save some tree-crickets chirping in the woods.

"You must be mistaken, Zimri," said Horton.

"Let us ride forward a few rods, captain, away from the troop. We can hear better then."

"Yes, I can hear them distinctly," Zimri continued, as he dismounted and placed his ear to the ground.

Although Horton followed the example of this keen-eared scout, yet he could not distinguish the slightest sound.

"Captain, there is a large party of them coming this way, and, from their direction, they must be rebels. If you will pardon me, sir, you can ride forward a little, and halt in the woods yonder. I will go on ahead, and will find out in a few moments who they are."

"Baxter shall go with you. But you have no arms."

"I can do much better alone, if you will let Baxter take care of my horse. As for arms, I don't need them just now. I shall find them when I want them."

In an instant the tall form of Zimri was running swiftly up the road, and soon disappeared in the shadow of the trees, while Horton followed him with his troop of soldiers, halting in an undergrowth of young trees which had sprung up under the shadows of the tall pines.

Five minutes could not have elapsed when Zimri again stood almost breathless by Horton's side. A new light shone in his pale face—an almost joyful look, which transformed those careworn features.

"Yes, captain, there is a regiment of rebel cavalry within three hundred yards of us, and they are coming along without suspicion of your presence. Oh, captain!" he exclaimed, with fervor, "thank God I can at last meet them in honorable battle. Oh, sir, I can now strike a blow in the cause of freedom.".

Horton turned to the troop, and said in low but distinct tones,

"Take the horses to the right and rear. Look well, men, to your carbines and cartridge-boxes. Preserve entire silence. Let not a word be spoken."

XXXIV.

WE will go back a few hours in the order of time, and enter the rebel lines. A council of generals has been called to attempt to restore the morale of the flying army, to decide upon some plan by which to check the progress of the Federal host. There is no unity in defeat, and wild and stormy is the debate; but upon one point they are all agreed: the invading foe are marching upon the vitally important railroad junction at Charlotte.

"If he can be drawn up into the mountains, we can attack his columns in detail, and destroy this cursed Yankee rabble," said one.

"For a rabble, they manage successfully to overrun our fortifications and capture our cities," said another, in a sneering tone.

"Would to Heaven President Davis would give up the useless defense of Richmond, and concentrate our armies in the interior," bitterly growled a third.

"This discussion is unnecessary, and divides our council, gentlemen," said Beauregard; and then, turning to Hampton, he continued—

"It is now near midnight. General, you will at once send a regiment upon the right flank of the enemy. Let them scout on all the roads, and, if possible, get in the enemy's rear, and penetrate their lines. A successful attack upon their wagon-train would be of more service than it is possible to attain if we oppose twenty times your number in their front. Send the best commanding officer you have."

In a few moments Hampton had issued his orders, and the regiment was in the road, marching quickly and confidently forward, for the Yankees were supposed to be far to the right of the route over which they were marching.

It was this body of cavalry whose footsteps had reached the quick ear of Zimri.

It was these reckless riders whom Horton was waiting to receive. He did not wait long.

XXXV.

THERE had been no moon that night, and at the moment when Horton halted his small command, it was near morning, and it was so dark that objects could not be defined ten yards ahead. A night fight is not the most pleasant of entertainments; but Horton had no choice in the matter of time. These people stood in his way to the river.

The rebel general was marching a few paces in the rear of his advance guard. They had passed a large plantation, and were just in the edge of the forest of lofty pines, while on either side of the road were old cotton-fields. Suddenly the guard halted. Riding forward, the general demanded,

"Why do you halt, sergeant?"

"I think I saw persons running across the road, in the woods there."

"Silence in the rear!" shouted the general to the

men, who were laughing and jesting with their usual recklessness of consequences.

In a moment the clamor ceased, and the only sound that broke upon the night air was the jingle of a sabre, as some restless horse moved about.

"You may have been in error, sergeant. Send forward your men to reconnoitre."

Hardly had the words escaped his lips when there came ringing through the forest the shrill neigh of a horse, which was answered by another and still another. With an oath the general shouted,

"We have struck the Yankee lines."

Turning quickly to his officer next in command, he cried,

"Dismount ten men at once, and throw down the rails on either side of the road. Deploy Company A to the right and Company B to the left, and form line of battle."

By this time the thick darkness was succeeded by a deceptive gloaming, in which loomed up, fifty yards in advance, spectral figures of horsemen with sabres drawn.

"Prepare to receive charge of cavalry!" shouted the general; and then, in the impetuosity of his fiery nature, in quick and sharp tones he cried,

"Prepare to charge; charge!"

The general, with two companies, dashed forward at the head of the column. From the Union side not a sound had followed the neighing of the horses. The silence was ominous.

In five seconds the rebel general was almost within sabre's touch of the line of horsemen in the wood, when they rapidly wheeled to the right and left (a single platoon of them only were there), and then there rang out above the clatter of arms, the tramp of horses, and the yells of the men, shrill and piercing, the single word "Fire!"

Streams of fire poured out from a hundred carbines, which radiated from the point in the road where the trap had been set toward the rebel lines. It was a most terrible cross-fire, where every shot told on either rider or horse. The road was filled with struggling, screaming, wounded, and dying men and animals.

From his position at the head of the column, the rebel general had escaped with a single companion. They found themselves in the open space beyond the woods, out from which came the rattle of musketry, the shouts of the combatants, the terrible screams of wounded horses.

"Are you hurt, Ghilson?" asked the general, turning to his companion.

"I think not, sir. This is an infernal ambuscade we have tumbled into."

"Yes, and only a light scouting party at that. This is not even an outpost, or we should see more troops coming up."

"What shall we do, general? How are we to get back?"

"By the way we came," replied the general, savagely, and he settled himself more firmly in the stirrups, while he pressed both spurs into the flanks of his horse, already maddened by the noise and conflict of battle. The noble animal sprang into the air, and bounded forward into the woods again, leaping over the fallen horses, trampling with his iron hoofs among the dead and dying, avoiding the showers of bullets.

In vain does Horton attempt to bar his passage. A cut from the flying sabre of the rebel rider disables his sword-arm.

"Capture or kill that man!" shouted Horton.

But he has run the gauntlet of death. He sees his soldiers, panic-stricken, flying from the field. A few strides of that noble horse have placed him beyond musket range. His companion is no longer by his side. With bitter curses he mutters,

"They may be rallied yet."

But a weird figure springs into the road before him—a tall, stalwart shape it is. His jacket is covered with dust and blood. Wild black eyes glare from behind the matted, tangled hair. The frightened horse leaps to one side in the attempt to pass; but an iron hand and an iron arm, impelled by an iron will, has gripped the bit, flaked with foam, and with prodigious strength holds the plunging beast as if he were chained to a rock.

The blooded stallion had felt that hand before. Horseman and footman recognized each other as well.

There were no words spoken by the two brothers except such language as may find speech in the eyes when Hate and Revenge give and accept the challenge of life for life. They are no longer master and slave, or, if they are, Zimri is master. Before General Ralph has raised his sword to strike, Zimri has loosened his hold of the bit, but at the same instant, with fingers of steel, he clutches the rider by the throat. The horse dashes away, but the rider remains. General Ralph was a superb horseman, but he lost his seat just then. He was well armed, but the muscles refused to obey the will. That relentless pressure of Zimri's fingers about his neck unnerved him. His sword fell harmless by his side.

There was justice and revenge in Zimri's fingers for Charlotte, his wife, twice murdered. The memories of a lifetime of outrages in bondage was in his fingers. This was more than the struggle for life as between man and man—more than that between the seducer and the betrayed husband. The spirit of Freedom had the spirit of Slavery by the throat, and meant to strangle it to death. It was that kind of equality which does not require special legislation, but has its abiding power in the fact that it asserts itself. It was that terrible power which, with the consciousness of newborn freedom, springs into life full armed, and woe be to him who menaces that liberty, and seeks to re-enslave.

The slave-master struggled hard, grappling with his enemy. At last they went down together in the road, and then, by a superhuman effort which men in the supreme crisis of death sometimes make, General Ralph freed his throat from Zimri's fingers. Springing to his feet, he drew a pistol from his belt. It was his last effort, for the life had gone out of him. He swayed to and fro, while Zimri stood watching. The stare of death was in the rebel general's eyes, there was a rattle in his throat, and then, in accents of rage, anguish, and despair, he moaned, "Slave! O God! my wife! my child!" and fell his full length, a dead man.

How long Zimri stood, with arms folded, watching by the ghastly corpse, he did not know. But Horton, who meanwhile had sent back to camp a detail with the wounded, found the freed man standing there.

"Zimri! Zimri! are you wounded? How came you here? Who is this dead man?"

Zimri, aroused from his stupor, with a piteous sadness in his face, looked at his questioner, and then at the figure lying in the dust.

"That man was General Ralph Buford, my half-brother; he called himself master."

"The husband of Mrs. Buford, at Winnsboro'?"

"Yes."

"Yes, I killed that man," he continued, in answer to the horrified inquiring look of Horton. "But it was a fair fight. He had no right, neither did he ask mercy from me. My father was his father, but if I thought his vile blood ran in my veins, I would let it out with my life."

Zimri did not need to defend the taking of the rebel general's life. Horton had witnessed too many scenes where friends and brothers met in deadly strife upon the battle-field. It was the mad declaration of the rebel general's wife which rang in his ears like a weird prophecy. Was it a chance coincidence, or was it a prophetic vision photographed to her senses at the moment? And whether truly or falsely, she had avowed her willingness for such a sacrifice.

Horton was not a believer in what is vulgarly called the supernatural, yet his temperament was imaginative, and imbued with that fine artistic sense which recognizes, if it does not comprehend, the mystery of the unseen. In the hour of battle a man lives out the history of years of peace. In this struggle for mastery of muscle and mind, the powers of the soul are sublimated to the supremest heights of thought. How grand were the brief moments just passed—the suspense before the shock of conflict, the wild thrill when steel met steel, the exultation of victory, and now the lifeless body of Buford, with bloodshot eyes, staring up into the misty gray of the morning. With vivid intensity Horton recalled that vision of the imagination which came up before him when standing among the solemn death-shadows upon the parapet of Fort McAllister, and again while the army rested at Savannah.

What possible relation was there between the revelation of death to Mrs. Buford and his own weird dreams?

XXXVI.

HORTON, without farther obstruction, reached the river. In a few hours he had made a thorough examination of the principal fords, and was able to report to his chief in ample time for him to make use of this invaluable information.

A momentous day was that for Sherman's army. With a grandeur and certainty of purpose comparable only to the majestic movements of the celestial spheres, it had partially revolved upon its own axis. With head and trail of fire, resistless, terrible as the comet wanderers of the air, it had shot off on a tangent, reaching the river between the rising and the setting of the sun, as it were, at a single bound.

Like every movement by the flank, this was in the highest degree dangerous, had there been a wise and active enemy in the front. But a demonstration by cavalry and infantry, vigorously made toward the north, confirmed the bewildered rebel leader in his mistaken suppositions, and it is probable that Sherman, that great hero of a host of heroes, never felt more secure against molestation than when he pitched his tents on the banks of the head-waters of the Santee.

There was the usual scene of bustle and excitement about the camp. Details of foraging parties, squads of mounted orderlies, and a small army of head-quarter negroes were hurrying to and fro from a neighboring barn, carrying bundles of fodder and sacks of corn. Fires were already burning in the rear of the tents, kettles of water were placed upon the blazing rails, camp-chests were emptied of their incongruous pharaphernalia of cooking utensils and table-ware. Prominent in this enlivening campaign was the *chef de cuisine*, a brawny negro, with his black arms buried in a huge mass of flour and dough, who was giving orders to his numerous attendants. He was king absolute: not even the commanding general might interfere here.

"Bob, wha fur yer stan' dar doin' nuthin'? Tak de fedders orf dat ar turkey!" was his angry cry to a juvenile darkey, who was inciting a gladiatorial exhibition between two roosters that day captured.

"Sam! Sam!" he shouted to another, "I gets tired a hollering arter you. Yer right dun lazy, yer is, an' dat's a fac'. When it comes ter eatin', yer mighty fas'. Now jes watch dat ar fire."

"Nigger," he continued, in a satisfactory growl to himself, "nigger is almost slower dan de poor white trash."

Under these energetic directions, dinner seemed in a fair way to be placed upon the covers of the camp-chest, which also was used as a table.

Other negroes were at work ditching about the tents, unpacking the blankets which served as mattress and covering for camp-beds.

The officers were grouped about variously employed, or waiting for dinner. Horton, under the surgeon's charge, was having his arm dressed, for the sword-cut of the rebel general had proved to be a more serious wound than he had at first supposed. While no blood was drawn, nor any bones broken, the upper part of the arm, from the shoulder to the elbow-joint, was swollen and inflamed, and the doctor pleasantly informed him that he must be careful, or disastrous consequences might follow.

Meanwhile the troops were going into camp. The army that day had been well "closed up," as the military phrase has it, when one brigade or a division marches close in the rear of another, and there are none of those widely separated gaps which oftentimes occur through straggling or a bad state of the roads. Column after column, as they approached the river, filed off to the right and left to their selected camping-grounds, their small shelter-tents, like scattered snow-flakes which fall in the autumn days, covering the hill-tops, spreading out over the meadows, nestling in the valleys.

Horton, released from the surgeon's kind care, with his friend Dalton, lay on the grassy bank watching a column of troops as they passed with quickened gait, conscious that they were about to obtain that rest they so much desired after their long day's march. Sturdy, healthy fellows were they, merrily singing or jesting with each other as they jogged along. The mules and horses with their packs, their load of blankets, pots, pans, kettles, knapsacks, and what not, seemed to understand that they too were near their home for the night, the former braying loudly in hungry anticipation of food and drink.

In the rear of this heterogeneous, straggling crowd of four-footed camp-followers there came a number of poor creatures, prisoners and deserters from the rebel army, pale, wan, and sickly. Some were hatless, their uncombed hair hanging in yellow streaks over their faces and necks. Many were without coats, with miserable apologies for shirts wherewith to cover their nakedness. The most of them picked their toilsome way over the hard roads with bare and bleeding feet—more were dirty, all were wretched, woe-begone, spiritless.

As this band of unfortunates came in sight, Dalton rose to his feet and walked out toward the road, scanning their faces as they passed. A painful, repulsive sight it was, and, as they staggered by, Dalton turned to rejoin his friend, while there came into his kind, noble face that old look of weary disappointment. Day after day had he made that search; thousands of just such hungry faces and tattered forms had passed before his eyes. Often had he asked questions; now and then he thought he had obtained a trace of Harold, but the investigation had proved fruitless, until, finally, he had ceased to question. The thread had been lost, and still he did not despair. He was still resolved. To find tidings of his brother alive he prayerfully hoped, and if dead, at least he would know how and where he died.

"Oh no," he thought, "noble, generous, tender, loving Agnes had not nursed Harold back to life to have it so ignobly sacrificed."

And then the associations of these two, Agnes and Harold, which these weeks past, during every hour of the day, were companions in his highest aspiration, his tenderest emotions, came at that instant more vividly to his mind than ever before, bringing tumultuous love-longings, suffusing his eyes with tears, and he halted several feet from Horton, and turned his face away, for even his friend must not see this emotion.

The gang of prisoners had not yet turned the corner of the road behind which the column of troops had disappeared from sight, when a wild cry breaks out from their midst. It is a cry of hope, of joy, of recognition. A figure moves out from among this unhappy throng. As he stumbles toward the Union officer, he calls, with a sad plaint in his voice, in the pathos of fear lest he be forgotten,

"David! David! David!"

Dalton does not recognize that pallid face, that shrunken, tattered, tottering form; but the sound of that voice, those pleading tones, strike the key-note of a strain these four years silent. It sang of childhood, home, father, mother, sister, brother, and he sprang forward to meet him, crying "Harold! Harold!" to catch the fainting form in his strong arms, to bear him away to his tent, to pour into that sick, thirsting soul words of loving welcome.

Horton, who had recognized in Harold the deserter who came to the head-quarters in Columbia, proffered his assistance to Dalton, and then left them to the sacred joys of their final reunion.

It is more than a year since that glad day, but Harold has never told the story of his persecution and suffering. He shrinks from any allusion to that subject with unutterable horror. The terrors of the Spanish Inquisition had its parallel in America in this our nineteenth century. But the flag of the United States became a SANCTUARY to all the victims of treason and oppression.

XXXVII.

IN all the gamut of human sensations, there is none comparable to that where the soldier, returning from a long campaign, where he has been shut out from all intercourse with home or the outer world, except such as he may obtain through the discolored or distorted stories of the enemy's newspapers, when he at last receives the package of letters and messages accumulated for weeks or months. It is a singular, anomalous sensation, when pleasure and surprise are strangely mingled. He passes over one and another missive, eagerly seeking for some familiar handwriting or significant postmark. If the wished-for indication is found, it is hastily read, and then put aside for more careful perusal; others are glanced over and then thrown away.

It was a curious sight to see that party of officers on the balcony of a house in Goldsboro' one day late in March of 1865. The army, after leaving the Santee River, had made the march to Fayetteville, had fought two pitched battles, and now had arrived at the objective point of the grand campaign of the Carolinas. Although all of the *dramatis personœ* who were presented to the reader in the opening chapter of this story had taken active part in these eventful scenes, yet none had been killed or seriously wounded, and here they were again, after traversing hundreds of miles, safely reunited, and each intent upon gathering up those varied threads, some two months' broken, which bind the soldier to home and friends.

It was the work of but a few moments for Horton to run over the handful of letters which came to him. From them he gathered a résumé of the most important events that had occurred within the radius of his home circle. His father and mother were well, but each line of their letters was laden with anxiety.

"Dear mother," he wrote in reply, "do not make yourself unhappy about me. I have good food and drink, am well, and more than contented. There is not half the danger you imagine in campaigning, and, so far as my personal feelings are concerned, I never felt more secure against harm than when in the presence of this great army."

The effort of writing these words cost him severe physical torture, for, in spite of the protests of his surgeon, he had performed the same active duties in the field, day and night, as if he had never received the blow from the sword of the rebel general. By means of exposure and fatigue, an abscess had formed, with aggravated inflammation, and it had been a subject of serious discussion among the surgeons whether or not an amputation should be performed. But Horton was utterly unmindful of arm or abscess in the perusal of his friend Blauvelt's letters, and he was not a little surprised when he read,

"Why did you not write me from Savannah? If you received my letters directed to you at that place, I am sure you would have replied."

Horton thought for a moment. "I did answer his letter. Is it possible that it miscarried?"

He did not know that he had directed Blauvelt's letter to Kate Noble.

"No matter, my dear soldier boy," the letter continued, "your affair goes well. I say 'affair,' because I am now sure that there has been some understanding between Gray and Miss Noble which concerned you. For some purpose, the secret of which I have not yet solved, Gray is persistent in his injurious allusions to you. He never makes definite charges, but deals in the most biting sarcasms. He has an astonishing talent for insinuating a mean thing, without saying it outright. There is no tangible point which you can take hold of. For example, he remarked in the presence of Kate Noble (we were all out at Jamaica Plains, at Hale's, the artist's; the occasion was a musicale), 'they say that Horton has been breveted major and colonel. Isn't it singular that, after four years' service, he has not been wounded? It is his good luck, I suppose.'

"There was an unmistakable sneer in the closing remark, which grated harshly on the ear of us all. In a flash Kate Noble answered,

"'It was true manliness which took Captain Horton to the war. He will perform his whole duty, wherever it requires him to go. As to the soldier's chances of good or bad fortune, you, Mr. Gray, are hardly capable of judging.'

"Wasn't that splendid? You should have seen the blood as it rushed to her cheek, whose peculiar color was like that of a ripe peach in a basket of white roses, while her full blue eyes gazed steadily and fearlessly at the unabashed yet somewhat astonished Mr. Gray.

"For once Gray's lips were silent, for he evidently was unprepared and surprised at her reply, although there was a sinister expression in his eyes which I can only describe as diabolical. Meanwhile Miss Kate, in answer to a request from Dressell, joined him at the piano in an artistic rendering of one of Schuman's duets.

"Since that incident, which occurred some six weeks ago, Gray has been more guarded in what he says. For my part, I was astonished at the readiness of Kate Noble's reply. It seemed as if she had prepared herself for it—as if she had had some warning of Gray's intention and motives. Any way, it was a crusher.

"I suppose, now that Sherman has planted his army of veterans on Lee's flank, we shall have more large, but, I hope, decisive battles. Take good care of that precious body of yours. Of all your friends here, no one will be more glad to take you by the hand than your old comrade of the palette, brush, and sword, BLAUVELT."

"How like Kate Noble," thought Horton, as he finished the letter, and imagined the scene described by his friend Blauvelt. "Why have I ever submitted myself to these stupid forebodings, so untrue of Kate, so unworthy myself?" And Horton, collecting together his letters and newspapers, crossed the piazza toward Major Dalton with a lighter heart than he had known these many years. There was a star in the east which to his eyes glowed with exceeding brightness just then.

"Why, Dalton," he exclaimed, "you look as solemn as a Shawnee Indian. You have not received bad news, I hope? Your father and mother, are they well?" he continued, more seriously, as he noticed an open letter in his friend's hand.

"Thank you, Horton, they are all well at home; but I have received a letter from Mrs. Bright, at Savannah, which alarms me. She writes that at the time I was up the river, Miss Saumur left the city and went North in a New York steamer. Where or to whom she is gone Mrs. Bright does not seem to know. I have no fear for Agnes's safety, for she has cousins who live on the Hudson River, a short distance from New York City. She has gone there, I suppose, where she will be warmly welcomed, and find a home."

"It seems to me," answered Horton, "that you should be rejoiced that she has escaped from Savannah. With her earnest devotion to our cause, she could not have remained there without discomfort and annoyance. You are nearer to New York, my dear fellow, than to Savannah."

L

"That is all true, Horton. I am not disturbed that she has gone North, but because she supposed I would return to Savannah before we started on this last campaign. It was to escape me—'to fly from herself,' were her parting words; that thought stings me—the fear that I may lose her after all these trials. She may give me up; she may banish me from her mind more effectually than I did my love for her until the day we met her on the public street three months ago."

There is just this difference between you and Miss Saumur. You are a man, and she is a woman. I admit that if she were to act by the code which a heartless world has set up for us, you might never see her again; but she has proven herself to be one of those great souls which rarely visit this earth. More than all this, she loves you as few of us deserve to be loved, and that word "love"—Horton's mind's eye at this moment was filled with a vision of golden hair, red cheeks, and blue eyes—will overcome greater difficulties than could this grand army, with Sherman at its head."

"Your kind words are full of encouragement, Horton. I wish to Heaven I had more of your enthusiastic, sanguine temperament."

"You must remember, major, that we were not born in the same latitude by several degrees."

XXXVIII.

IT was in the last days of May, 1865, that Dalton and Horton, on leave of absence, were enjoying what is a peculiar sensation for those who for years have known no swifter means of locomotion than upon horseback. They were traveling northward by an express train, which sped swiftly over the iron rails, but not too quickly for our furloughed soldiers. The war was ended, and with peace came temporary release from duty. Horton and Dalton were both promoted to the rank of colonel by brevet. The two officers were accompanied by Zimri, who, since the night of the cavalry fight, had been the inseparable attendant of Horton. Harold was also one of the party. Upon the arrival of the army at Goldsboro', Dalton had at once telegraphed to his parents the good news of the discovery of the son and brother, who, by the way, would not now have been recognized as the ragged, sickly rebel prisoner whom we saw on the banks of the Santee. The two brothers expected to find their parents at New York, which had been appointed as a place of rendezvous. For Dalton the great metropolis had a yet more thrilling interest; for, although he had received no token of Agnes Saumur since the letter from Mrs. Bright, yet he did not permit himself for a moment to doubt but what he should find her again; and then—but beyond that he dared not even hope.

We will leave the two brothers for the present, and follow Horton as he enters the city of his birth and manhood's early days. His first duty was to his good old father and fond mother, proud of their noble son. Their tears of sacred joy, the thankful prayer mingled with tears, may not be intruded upon here. Only those whose days and nights for long years have been passed in heart-aching fears and hopes, who with fainting heart read each battle-list of wounded and slain, can know the inexpressible gladness when the absent one returns to their arms again.

The well-remembered bell of the old South Church tolled nine o'clock as Horton took the road to the residence of Kate Noble. The sound brought back a thousand recollections of childhood's days, of happy hours, whose good angel was the woman he had loved with a singleness of purpose second only to his devotion to the cause for which he had offered his life upon many a battle-field. As he passed along, his mind was filled with thronging, contending emotions, which he in vain attempted to analyze. While he was at the war, in spite of all his doubts and forebodings, he reveled in the wildest, most illimitable anticipations of future happiness when he should again see Kate Noble. Now that he had arrived at the point where his destiny was to be decided, he hesitated, and a disheartening timidity crept over him. He had seen soldiers who were very brave until they came within reach of the enemy's shot and shell, when they suddenly discovered that there were obstacles in the way between them and the fortification to be carried. These men were not afraid, but they lost heart sometimes.

But Horton was pressed forward by an incentive as powerful as that which ever animated his comrades upon the battle-field.

At the first thought there may not seem to be any analogy between love and war; but they resemble each other in this, that in both the grandest possibilities of human nature are called into action, although in love, especially with women, the desperate struggle comes when the grand passion demands the utter subordination of the personality to its decree.

XXXIX.

"MISS KATE is out, but will return presently," was the reply to his call.

"You do not recognize me, William?" he said to the gray-haired major-domo, who had been in the service of the Noble family long before Kate was born.

"Walk in, sir—come in. Why, God bless my soul! yes, it is Mr. Horton. Indeed, we are glad to welcome you home, sir. You've grown older, sir. You have been wounded, haven't you? Your arm is in a sling. Nothing serious, I hope. We have not heard you were wounded. Come into the library, Mr. Horton—Colonel, I mean. We saw your promotion in the papers. Miss Kate will be glad to see you, and so will Mr. Noble. He talked a deal about you, sir; is rather proud of his protégé—that's what he calls you. Sit in the big chair, colonel. There are the papers. Indeed, you are looking finely, sir," and the garrulous, good-natured old man would have run on to an indefinite extent, but Horton arrested the flow of kind words.

"Thank you, William, I am well otherwise than the arm, which might be worse, and glad to get home again. I won't detain you. Oh, William, if any one returns with Miss Kate, please not say that I have arrived. They won't be likely to come in here, and I don't care to see strangers to-night."

"I'll remember, colonel" (the old man dwelt upon the title); "but you are the last gentleman we expected to see. It looks like old times to see your face," and the old man left the room.

In order the better to understand the events which subsequently occurred, it is necessary to describe the situation. The big arm-chair in which Horton was enveloped was placed in a large alcove of the library, which was also a bay-window looking out upon a garden attached to the house. This was Kate's favorite seat, as it was of any one who ever received its capacious embraces. The library was one of a suite of rooms upon the ground floor of the building. In the rear was the dining-room. The front apartment, looking upon the street, was used as a reception-room.

Horton had hardly renewed his acquaintance with

the old arm-chair, when the hall door opened, and he could hear Kate's rich, full voice, whose tones thrilled him with a restful gladness, the joy of compensation, a reward only those know who have loved and waited.

"Come in, Louise, and I will give you that duet, which you can practice at your leisure."

Horton recalled to mind that Louise Gray, the sister of his former friend, was the intimate friend of Kate. She was a girl of a simple, unpretending nature, but truthful and conscientious. These endearing qualities, and an ardent passion for music, had brought about between the two girls a close intimacy. But Horton was not so well pleased when he heard the voice of Gray in response.

"Run in, Louise; it is early in the evening, and we can wait until Miss Kate finds the music."

Horton, from his alcove, could hear distinctly every word of the conversation. While he was entirely concealed from view, he could follow every movement of Kate as she laid aside her hat and cloak. He could hear Gray move a chair to the fire; and when he sat down, Horton's impulse was at once to rise and reveal himself; but a reluctance, which was proper and natural, to exchange the first greetings with Kate in another's presence, and, of all persons, this man Gray—this repugnance held him to his seat. He might have acted otherwise could he have anticipated what was to follow.

"A pleasant concert we had this evening," said Gray.

"Yes," answered Kate, "it was pleasant. But I was not in a mood for musical enjoyment to-night. The glorious news of the surrender of Johnston's army, and the certainty that peace is once more to bless the land, filled up all my enjoyable powers."

"Yes, it is gratifying. I suppose we shall be overrun with shoulder-straps in a few days," replied Gray.

"They will be glad to come home after their hardships and dangers," replied Kate, "and welcome comers they will be. I never see one of the commonest looking soldiers that I am not inspired with the deepest feelings of respect and admiration for what they have dared and suffered for the cause of liberty."

At that moment Horton would not have exchanged his uniform for an emperor's robes.

"You were always romantic, Miss Kate," said Gray. "For my part, I am tired of these bars, and eagles, and stars."

As she handed Louise the roll of music, there was

a malicious, defiant look in Kate's eyes which would have silenced a man of less assurance than Gray. His first remark had excited her indignation, as she knew he intended it should, and she had resolved not to give him any advantage of the kind.

"I do not understand why these insignia of honor should annoy you so much. Surely your shoulders have never been burdened with them."

Kate's answer went home to the weakest spot of Gray's mental diaphragm, and it was made with a coolness and determination which completely broke down his guard. A black cloud passed over his face as he rose from his seat and stared Kate full in the eyes.

"I suppose you are looking for Horton's arrival in a few days?"

"Yes," replied Kate, calmly, "and I shall be very glad to see him when he does return."

There was silence for a few moments, and then Gray advanced to where Kate stood.

"Miss Kate, I have told you again and again that Horton is not worthy of any woman's love. I have given you proofs of his weakness. He is not capable of love. I supposed you were satisfied of this."

"Oh, Henry," interrupted his sister, "you have no right to speak so unkindly of Mr. Horton."

"Louise," answered Gray, impatiently, "I won't permit you to interfere in this matter. You know, and Kate understands, that I am her best friend, and only speak for her good."

"Mr. Gray, I did once believe that you were my friend, but you pretended to be the friend of Captain Horton. Heretofore I listened to you, but I never for one instant lost faith in him. For some reason which I can not explain, you have sought to degrade him in my eyes. Thank Heaven you did not succeed. I know him to be a true-hearted, brave gentleman. It was shameful of you to slander a man whom you should have defended instead of abused. I will not listen to you again. You never had the right to speak to me—to "warn me," as you term it. It was a presumption which never was justifiable, even by the association which brought us together, through my love for Louise. I should have resented it long ago."

Kate did not dare to charge Gray with the real motives which she suspected had been the cause of his dislike of Horton. It is rare, indeed, that a woman is not conscious when a man loves her. While Gray had proffered the most disinterested friendship, which for years had taken form in kindly attentions, yet her intuitions told her that all the while a deeper feeling lay beneath, which Gray would have called love, and that he only waited the lightest word or look from her to give it breath. That encouragement she had never given, never could give, for an irresistible aversion had taken the place of her old-time friendship for him, and if it had not been for the love she bore Louise, she would long since have freed herself from a relation which was fruitful only of pain and chagrin.

If Horton had at first been reluctant to meet Kate in the presence of others, the course of the conversation had now rendered it impossible. The situation was especially painful to him, who hated any word or act which savored of concealment; but here he was, fixed in this easy-chair, which had now become a seat of thorns. Meanwhile Louise had walked out into the hall, calling to her brother,

"Henry, I beg of you to come home. We have staid too long already."

"I will follow you in a moment," was the answer, and then Horton could hear the low, but clear-sounding words which followed, in a tone of threatening and of accusation,

"Kate Noble, I believe you love Horton."

The colonel half started to his feet. In the impulse of his honest indignation, under any circum-

"And then Horton, from the darkness of the library, entered into the full light of the reception-room."

stances he would have resented this shameful outrage upon every sense of womanly delicacy and manly honor, but he sank back in his seat as Kate's dignified answer came forth, quick and strong:

"You have no right to say this, whether or not it be true. You have violated all sense of manliness. It was cowardly. Leave me, Mr. Gray, and never speak to me again."

There was no appeal from this decree, for Kate stood there with burning eyes fixed upon the false friend and would-be lover until, abashed and condemned, he slunk away out of the room and out of the house.

And then Horton, from the darkness of the library, entered into the full light of the reception-room. Kate was standing by the mantle, her head gently inclined forward as she gazed into the fire. Her indignation had already given place to another and more pensive mood. The sound of footsteps aroused her, and she turned, startled and almost alarmed, to see the figure of Horton, who had halted midway in the room, unable to speak, unable to move farther.

To Kate there was something strange in that erect, soldierly form, that face bronzed by exposure. In the close-cut hair, the drooping mustache, and long imperial, she did not for the moment recognize the light form and ruddy face which had bid her adieu years ago, and which had been enshrined in her heart. It was a deity she had worshiped with all the devotion of a nature which was all the more beautiful in its romantic enthusiasm because secluded and repelled by the cynical conventionalities of the society about her.

If Kate was confused for an instant by this sudden appearance — if Time and War's rough hand had wrought such changes in Horton's exterior, the deception was but for an instant, for the soldier-lover's eyes were speaking more eloquently than could tongue of silver, and then, like some full orchestral strain of heavenly music, the truth entered into her heart and soul. The hero of her day-dreams and visions of the night had come back; he stood before her. In these imaginings she had pictured this hour of meeting, and how quietly she would receive him. She would test his love. But, in the first impulse of gladness, she forgot all these resolutions of maidenly reserve. The pathetic appeal of the wounded arm resting in its sling, the earnest, magnetic brown eyes, love-beseeching, broke down all barriers. With a passionate trembling, which vibrated through heart and body, she stretched forth her arms in mute welcome. In a moment Kate, without well knowing how it came about, found her head resting upon his shoulder; his arm encircled her, holding her throbbing heart close to his; his lips pressed to hers with passionate fervor, with that inexpressible tenderness which has no *arrière pensée*—that first kiss when two souls, in the fullness of long waiting, take possession of each other.

"My heart has not deceived me then, Kate, during these long years of absence?"

"I can not remember when I did not love you, Alfred, but I never was so gladly assured of your love as when I received a letter which you wrote at Savannah, and evidently misdirected to me."

Horton at once remembered his blunder, and now understood the meaning of Blauvelt's letter which he had received at Goldsboro'.

"I do not regret that you received the letter intended for Blauvelt, although it was written in the anger of my pride—the pride of loving, Kate. You have been my good angel, darling, from the first. My hopes, my faith, were centred in you. The pains, the dangers, the glories of my soldier-life are crowned by the bliss of this possession," and Horton kissed away the tears of joy which filled Kate's eyes.

"I am very happy, Alfred—happier than the happiest; for"—she hesitated a little, while there was a rebellious twinkle in her bright eyes—" at one time I had reason to believe you unfaithful, and—".

"I was an unintentional listener, Kate, to the treacherous declarations of that man Gray. But anger, darling, can not enter this heaven. We will forgive, if we can not forget his baseness. I have won honor and fame, Kate, but until this moment I have never prized these laurels, for now I can wreath them among these golden tresses," and he passed his hand gently through the luxurious mass of flowing hair.

XL.

THE afternoon of the arrival in New York of Major Dalton and his brother was spent in a reunion of the family. A warm greeting did they receive. Harold could scarcely recognize in the elegant young lady who wound her arms about his neck his little sister Nelly. A happy meeting was this, where no cloud of misfortune cast its saddening shadow. How many similar scenes might have been witnessed in those days when the triple wall of prejudice, hate, and armed resistance was thrown down, and the North and the South were no longer the North and the South, but one common country!

Dalton had not yet received any tidings of Agnes. This much he knew, that her cousins, the Marcys, usually passed but a few weeks of the winter season in town, and that their country place was situated not far from a village on the Hudson River.

It was too late to attempt to go up the river that

day. Dalton was restive and ill at ease. He could not curb the impatience of his reawakened love, which every hour more and more loudly demanded justification. To see Agnes—to prove to her that he had never lost his love for her—that his coldness at Savannah was but a natural exhaustion after four years of war's excitement—to show her that he loved her with all the fervor and truth which her grand nature demanded — this was the burden of his thoughts.

It was after nightfall, when walking up and down the streets of the city, that these and a thousand suggestions and plans came jostling tumultuously through his mind. As he passed along, a poster informed him that the opera of the "Huguenots" was to be performed that night. Here was food—distraction for the moment, at least.

As Dalton settled himself into his seat in the parquette, the house commenced to fill. From his place at the end of the dress-circle, and between that and the stage-boxes, he could see the crowd of people as they came in by one and another entrance. A novel sight it was to him. Beautiful women, in all the glory of their womanhood, decked in brilliant toilets, fluttered to their places like rose-leaves deflowered by the summer wind. Like a garden full of pink, and violet, and crimson flowers were they, and set in frames of white and gold. First, the parterre blossomed out a bed of lilies, fuchsias, and carnations. Here a knot of volatile French people are wonderfully busy talking; behind him sits three Cubans, olive-skinned, dark-eyed; a German, with his wife, has obtained a place near the stage; English, Irish, and Italian—all nations of the earth are represented here. On the other side of the aisle a young girl makes room for her lover to pass, looking up into his face with undisguised delight. That look means nothing else than love, and he answers it with a smile.

Respectable old gentlemen, with aged companions, sink into their fauteuils, not to rise again until the end of the performance. A platoon of country people file into the seats in front. The leader of the squad has a clerical air, and looks about with a guilty manner, as if he feared the eye of some stern parishioner was upon him. But a sense of duty sustains him and his fellows. They must know by experience against what sins to warn their flock.

A party of children rush into one of the upper boxes, perching upon the balustrade, chirping and twittering like gay birds in the sunshine. And now the orchestra comes tumbling in, or up rather, out from a hole under the stage. They are the artillery of the *corps dramatique*, and as they wander to their places, in and out among harps, and drums, and music-stands, they stare out across the sea of human faces and up into the galleries, as a sailor, when he first comes on deck, takes a look at the tossing waters and cloud-flecked sky, to see what the signs of the weather are.

The second tier of boxes are now slowly filling up with the *beau monde*—the later comers. A fine display they make in silks, and satins, and costly parures. And now the stragglers of this army are gathering on the flank and rear of the camp, content with such resting-place as their feet may find, provided always they are in at the feast of sight and sound.

The amphitheatre, that refuge of moneyless critics, has a long time been filled. Indeed, the vast interior of this grandest opera-house of all the world is surcharged and o'ertopped with a smiling, murmuring mass of humanity.

One of the *jeunesse dorée*, perfumed and polished, dances to a seat by the side of the stern young soldier. With lavender-gloved hand he gently pats his delicate whiskers, while a simpering smile of conscious irresistibility flickers faintly over his insipid features as he stares into the box near by. A lady has entered there, startled, and with a glad look in her face. She stands gazing—the dandy thinks at him.

Exceedingly beautiful she is. A figure erect and queenly, with wondrous grace and dignity. A dress of pearl-gray silk fits close to her form. A trimming of delicate lace borders the neck and sleeve. There are no diamonds nor gems about her. She needs none.

The head rests gracefully upon her faultless neck. The skin is a rich brunette, and the mass of wavy dark hair is relieved by a single flower — a rose just bursting into blossom. The eyes are large, and of that luminous black, from whose unfathomable depths there plays a soft, mysterious light. The forehead is uneven, with arched brows, which lends a grace to the oval outline of the face. The chin is finely rounded, but firm, and just now the finely-cut lips are parted, as if about to speak.

A murmur of admiration wanders over the parquette. The *habitués* ask one another, Who is this new-comer? Lorgnettes from every part of the house, even in feminine hands, are leveled at her as she stands there, all unconscious of this homage paid to beauty, for her eyes, now grown preternaturally bright, are fixed upon Dalton. The major, in dreamy listlessness, is gazing at the throng.

"Cousin Agnes," said a lady who had advanced into the box, "are you aware you have attracted the attention of the audience?"

A flush of crimson mounted to the young girl's face as she raised her eyes, and she quietly took the seat which was offered her.

At that instant Dalton turned his head to ascertain the cause of the excitement throughout the house, but he was too late. He could only see a small, elegantly-gloved hand resting upon the cushion of the rail. A white lace shawl falling over swept his face and shoulder. The figure of its owner was within reach of his hand, but she was facing the stage, and away from him. An indistinct sound of voices reached his ear, a fragrance filled the air such as he had known before, he could not tell where nor when; yet his curiosity, if so much interest had been aroused as would justify the use of the word, was very soon diverted, for the *chef d'orchestra* had raised his baton, the vast audience was subsided into silence, and then those sublime harmonies of Meyerbeer's masterpiece rose and fell, now filling the air with bursts of martial music, now sinking into gentlest melodies, and again swelling in strains of religious fervor.

Major Dalton was unable to observe the occupants

of the box by his side, but Agnes Saumur, as she sat there, could see reflected in the mirror on the opposite wall every expression of feeling, every light and shade of thought which animated the face of the man whom, at that moment, she loved as she had never loved him before—the face she had not seen since that day of tearful memories on the river's bank by her mother's grave. In the long years of loving, she had studied every line and every character of those features, until, with more than woman's intuition, she could interpret his inmost thought and motive. To her, the exterior was the casting, the type from the mould within. The story it told her only a few months ago was mournful proof of her powers; and now eagerly did she gaze into that countenance, manly and resolute as of old, yet softened and gentler than ever before.

Agnes was familiar with the music of the Huguenots. The story was one that touched her closely, for her ancestors had suffered in those cruel persecutions for opinions' sake. Indeed, many of them, survivors from the cowardly massacre of St. Bartholomew, had fled to America. When a child, seated upon the knee of her grandfather, she had listened with bated breath to legends of peril and death to those religious martyrs.

M

In the music and story of the play there was a romance, a unity, and grandeur of dramatic power which had triple force this night. The music of Meyerbeer, perhaps more than any other dramatic composer, tells its own story; and Agnes did not care to witness the action of the singers; she could revel in the delight of seeing with Dalton's eyes.

This was no magic mirror into which she was gazing; no conjuror's wand peopled its polished surface, and yet it all seemed like a phantasm, a dream.

As the curtain rose, the chorus of revelers rang out their boisterous bacchanalian song, and then came the stern old Huguenot, defiant and grand, describing the skirmish, the musket-shot, the rush of the fight; and then, as some lofty monument rears its head from out the noise and littlenesses of the bustling city, so the Lutheran chant poured forth its sublime protest against the frivolities of the godless wine-drinkers.

And Dalton's kind eyes sparkled with pleasure when Miss Phillips, an acquaintance of long years, appeared as the page. The very embodiment of grace and art, she trilled forth, in rich contralto tones, the merry "No, no, no."

And then the imposing pageant of the court, with festooned barge and blatant trumpetings, passed away; and when the concourse of cavaliers and fanatic priests raised high the sword and cross, and swore the assassin's oath, a shock of pain passed over the brave soldier's face. He had felt the malign influence of that wicked intolerance which reproduces itself in every age and people. Following fast in heavenly contrast, Valentine sighs forth the confession of love, forced from her in fear for Raoul's safety. In all the world of art, where is there a more perfect picture of the intense abandon of love? It has been immortalized by Millais's inspired pencil; but that which language, nor pen, nor pencil can express, finds utterance in this incomparable duet, the triumph of nature, the sublimation of art.

But the signal-bell summons Raoul from love to duty.

How keenly did the patriot Southerner sympathize with the struggle between the lover and the man. As Agnes divined his thoughts, a pang of remorse swept over her with the memory that she had deserted him in his hour of trial.

"But have I not been punished?" she asked herself. "Have I not atoned for that weakness?"

But no thought of censure entered Dalton's mind. Beneath the reserve of his nature, which seemed cold and haughty at times, there were all the generous impulses, the keen susceptibilities, the passionate emotions of the Southern race. Removed so long from the esthetical refinements of life, an actor in the rough, stern realities where men make history, and, since the interview with Agnes at Savannah, pressed forward by a torrent of passionate emotion, he came into the presence of this divine world of sound a plastic creature of love, and thus he opened his heart and soul, and let the flood of music flow in and take possession of his entire being. In the story of the Huguenots there was so much of his own and Agnes's life that he was lost, as it were, in the absorption of this one great heart-passion. And when the curtain rose upon the final scene, and the two lovers, kneeling in the presence of Death, with exquisite melody sang the last sad song of love, Dalton, with his own sad longings, could bear no more, and turned his moistened eyes from the scene. And Agnes at the same instant, animated by the same emotion, unmindful of the place, conscious only that Dalton was there, that he sincerely loved her, half rose from her seat, turned, and the lovers were face to face.

"Agnes!"

"David!"

Electrified, they gazed each in the other's eyes.

In the moment of silence which followed, there was sanctified between David Dalton and Agnes Saumur that perfect marriage of the soul, all-comprehending, eternal.

Amid the crashing of drums and trumpets, and the discharge of muskets, Dalton saw Agnes, and only Agnes. Her voice only reached his ear—

"Bellevue, to-morrow"—

and she had disappeared. Dalton wished to follow, but the curtain had fallen. In vain did he search through the crowd. Agnes could not be found.

XLI.

"THE road is a crooked one, and you will have trouble in finding Bellevue," said the rather solemn-looking dépôt-master, in answer to Dalton's inquiry.

"What is the general direction? If you can give me that, I have no doubt but I can find the place."

"Yes, yes. You know where Dr. Braxton lives?"

"No; I am a stranger here."

The good man looked curiously at the half-military costume of his questioner, while he seemed surprised that any one could be a stranger in Bellevue —to him it was all the world—and that so intelligent a man as Dalton appeared to be should not know where the famous author of "Wealth and Its Uses" resided. After a moment of perplexed thought, he continued, pointing to the broken line of hills which rise from the river's bank in abrupt but picturesque forms,

"Do you see the white marble house which lies east of the old Albany road?"

"Yes, I see the building, if you mean that one with the tower and gable-ends."

"Exactly. Well, the Marcys live a few hundred yards beyond. The house is back from the road apiece, with trees in front, and granite gate-posts at the entrance. If you are not afraid of getting lost, you can cut across country, and save a deal of walking."

"Thank you for the information," replied Dalton; "I should prefer a walk over these hills to tramping in the dusty roads."

Dalton was no novice in the art of crossing country. In campaigning, the roads are not always the most comfortable nor the safest route of travel.

It was a bright sunny morning, and as Dalton left the cluster of houses near the station and climbed the steep hills, it seemed to his elated senses as if Nature never had appeared more beautiful. Accustomed as he was to the wide-spreading, monotonous savannas, the low marsh-lands of the South, and the rank luxuriance of its tropical vegetation, there was an inexpressible charm in the rugged character of the scenery which now rose up before him.

A heavy shower of rain of the night before had

started into life myriad buds, and blossoms, and leaves. There was a novel beauty in this foliage which now greeted his admiring eyes for the first time—in the rough rocks covered with moss and lichens—in the hardy pine and cedar, the birch and maple, springing from the crevices of ledges which appeared to find their base in the eternal foundations of the earth.

As he passed along, bounding from rock to rock, plunging into the woods, traversing the fields, his feet seemed to take buoyancy from his heart, elastic with the joy of love. All nature was in grand accord with the one key-note of his delighted consciousness. The wrens and thrushes, flitting among the branches, caroled one name; the orange-breasted oriole had borrowed its richest tints from her cheek; the delicate-stemmed columbine, clinging to its rocky bed, bowed its lovely head in homage to her grace; the modest violet hid its purple leaves among the sedgy grasses in gentle recognition of her chaste presence.

Dalton mounted the hill-sides, and crossed the rivulets, which dashed merrily over their pebbly beds. The fields spread forth their carpets of green, decorated with wild flowers, where tufts of coltsfoot, in sober gray, were coyly kissing the full-stalked genarious, and dandelions mingled their golden petals with the succulent red-topped clover, and the yellow buttercups were drinking in full draughts of sunlight. Beds of forget-me-nots nodded kindly welcome to the young lover; pale-eyed anemones looked out upon him from their shady nooks; the lilies of the valley joined in the hymn of love, shaking tremblingly their silver bells; while white dragon's-teeth and the crimson honeysuckle whispered of gentle rest.

A countless host of verdurous beauties were these — an invading army of white and green, whose thousand banners of blue, and red, and yellow were gently waving in the wind, surging over the hill-tops, and walls, and fences—a host armed with shield and spear, riotous with its new-born life, with its squads of wild pinks, like skirmishers in the extreme advance, clinging to the edges of the granite cliffs. And thus, in all their pride and glory, flanked on either side by blossoming hedge and sturdy forest-trees, the troops of flowers moved on, chanting the song of love and spring-time.

The fragrance from peach and apple blossoms floated in the air from orchards nestling in the valleys; beds of wild strawberry at his feet gave forth their delicate perfume, and the violet contributed its fragrant incense to the offering upon love's altar. The dingy cedars, like bachelors who have outlived the summer and winter time of love, looked sadly down upon the young shoots, the budding trees, the tender leaves; but in the contrast, these countless objects of beauty just springing into life were all the more charming.

To Dalton all this wealth of form and color had but one interpretation; to him it was significant of glad promises, and his brain reeled with these intoxicating sights and odors of fecundating nature. It was the full spring-time, and every object was eloquent with the language of love. It was the season of hope, of desire, of promise.

As Dalton approached the summit of the hills, here and there, through the openings of the trees, he caught glimpses of the river, dotted with white sails, and beyond a faint line of azure, which marked the distant mountains, or the gray walls of the palisades lifted themselves beyond the leaves and branches. Cabinet gems were these in a panorama of ever-changing beauty. Now and then he passed splendid villas—"palaces" they would have been called in the Old World—and once his way led near a vineyard resting upon a sunny slope, where the happy husbandman was trimming the sprouting vines.

As Dalton proceeded on, he found he had come into a pathway which led out upon a terrace. To his right, through the trees, he could see a flower-garden, and beyond the wide piazza of a house. To his immediate left was a wall, which not only served as a line of demarcation, but which prevented the earth from sliding a hundred feet into the road below, which, glittering in the sunlight, seemed like a thread of gold winding its way under the willows and elms, and over the hills, until lost in the mazes of "Sleepy Hollow." A glorious sight it was which spread out before his eyes, as he gazed to the northward over meadow, field, and forest to the Hudson, widening out into the broad Tappan Zee, dotted with sail, and steamer, and raft, and barge — its shores basking in the sunlight—its promontories crowned with castellated mansions—its bank bordered with villages—and then, beyond, the mountains melting into the pale blue sky. To the west, the Palisades bounded the horizon—that wall of granite, stretching to the sea, which in the dawn of creation lifted its majestic front from out the seething waters—emblem of eternal might in its grandeur and simplicity.

And Dalton stood spellbound as his eye wandered over this scene of incomparable beauty. Nowhere in all the world can be found so rare a combination of the grand and picturesque. Not on the Rhine, with its vine-clad hills and ruined castles—not on the shores of that mountain lake immortalized by the loves of a Heloise—not in the Old World nor the New is there a vision so full of witching grace, of human interest, of the sublime, the eternal.

Inspired with a sense of reverential awe and infinite tenderness, the impassioned Southerner realized in his inmost nature the inspired words of the Evangelist, "God is Love."

With love's prophetic intuition, he was certain he should find Agnes out in the open air.

"Was she not queen of all this vision of beauty? and should she not move in the presence of her subjects?"

Advancing toward an arbor of flowering vines perched upon the edge of the terrace, Dalton suddenly found himself within a few feet of this queen of his dreams.

Agnes did not expect Dalton to come by the pathway which led through the wood. All the morning she had gazed down the road, and over the roof of green, and out upon the waters, over which the clouds were flinging their purple shadows, and then her eyes wandered back upon the road again. Not for a moment did she doubt his coming. She had gone forth to meet him with a heart light and joyous, yet tempered with that strange sadness which comes with perfect peace in loving.

Never had she appeared more beautiful to her lover than now. Her robe of lilac and rose, her dark hair relieved against the pure skin, blooming with the freshness of the morning, she had that fresh delicacy which we admire in the leaves when first unfolding from the bud.

It was a tremulous, broken cry of ecstatic joy which came from her lips when Dalton stood before her, and she ran to his open arms and nestled to his heart. Oh the ineffable bliss of that moment, when every sense, all consciousness, was lost in the resistless flood. In its noontide glory Dalton was transfigured to the Psalmist's conception of the "full stature of a man;" and Agnes was all woman now, for absolute faith and absolute trust filled up the measure of her love.

Never were two natures more harmoniously united than were these. In one as in the other, there was the same love of the beautiful, the same devotion to the right. Never were two souls more closely intertwined by mutual suffering than were theirs. From the wintry tears shed upon that lonely grave in Bonaventura had sprung, moistened into life, the bright flowers of an everlasting spring-time of love. It had been a trial of rectitude over self, and both had come out conquerors.

Gently as the golden clouds floated across the pure sky passed the hours, until the sun began to sink behind the Palisades, now a purple shadow looming up in gigantic proportions against the sky. Through narrow clefts in the distant hills the God of Day yet poured a flood of glory, illuminating some quiet village, or shooting broad bars across the crimson waters, transforming their smooth surface into a carpet of red and gold. And now the sun, a fiery disc in a sea of orange, and azure, and emerald, disappears from sight. The countless cloud-wavelets in the empurpled zenith give back in rosy hues its last rays, which linger like the flush on the cheek of the dying; and now even that is gone, and Agnes clings closer to her lover's breast. And then meadow, and field, and forest are covered by a misty veil; the birds have gone to rest; the hills have changed from russet to purple and blue; the distant mountains have vanished into night; the world of stars have come forth, and sparkle and glimmer in the heavens, reflected in multiplied beauties in the bosom of the river below. But, more beautiful than all, hanging in the western sky, radiant in virginal purity, Venus

"God is very kind to us, David."

beams forth—a sign of promise, emblem of eternal love.

The silence is hardly broken by Dalton's trembling words,

"Let us go in—the night air may chill you; the dew-drops already glisten in your hair, Agnes, darling—my wife."

"God is very kind to us, David."

XLII.

IT is certain that that highly respectable old gentleman, Mr. James Noble, never was so amazed as when, one day, Colonel Horton said to him,

"Mr. Noble, I wish to ask for your consent to the marriage of Miss Kate and myself."

The three—Kate, her father, and the colonel—had just retired to the library after dinner. We said that Mr. Noble was amazed, but this fails to express his astonishment. Here, for two weeks, Horton and Kate had been blooming in the sunshine of young love before his eyes, and not the faintest suspicion of the fact had found its way through the maze of contracts, statistics, and prices current which filled the worthy merchant's head. For want of words, he fixed his eye-glass to his nose, and stared at the young soldier. This optical demonstration necessarily included Kate; for with that brave heart and wisdom of a true soldier's wife which she was destined to be, she understood the value of putting in the reserves at the critical moment, and had taken position resting upon the colonel's left.

Mr. Noble had never studied Jomini nor Ovid, and was ignorant of the tactics of war or love, yet he could not misunderstand this movement. Without making any reply to Horton's request, he at last found words to address his daughter:

"Well, Kate, what does this mean? I—I—never dreamed of such a thing."

"I love him, father. I loved him a long while ago." And Kate wound her arm about her father's neck, while her disengaged hand was still held fast in Horton's.

"But, Colonel Horton," said the old gentleman, turning upon that resolute-looking young man, "how can you support a wife? You haven't any income. You are going to leave the army, you say, and you have no occupation."

"I have saved money from my pay, and I intend to follow my old profession as an artist. With the material which I have gathered during the war, I have no fear but what I can paint pictures which will insure me a competency."

"Humph!" was the response of the old gentleman, who thought of the amount which Horton might have saved out of $150 per month. The soldier's pay did not assume any large proportions in view of Mr. Noble's last speculation in cotton, which had netted him some $50,000.

"Well, well, we'll see about it," he said, as he left the happy lovers and set out for the club, muttering to himself as he walked along, "He's a thousand times better than these whipper-snappers who staid at home."

Not many months after this event, and but a few weeks ago, Horton and Kate were married in King's Chapel, to the delight of all who witnessed the ceremony, which did not include Henry Gray in the number. To Horton there is no such person as Henry Gray.

The fortunes of the other actors in our story may be quickly told.

Zimri is in charge of a Sea Island plantation, which is the property of Mr. Noble, where he fulfills his duties to the perfect satisfaction of all concerned. Zimri is where he would best love to be—among his own people, in whose moral and intellectual advancement his heart is bound up. Manly and gentle, tender even, he is to them; yet there never was a plantation under the old system conducted with more order or with greater economy.

Zimri Horton, for that is the name he bears, is what the world sometimes calls a broken-hearted man; that is, he carries with him an unutterable sadness. Life to him is no longer a joy, but a duty, and he bends himself to his work with unceasing endeavor. In work only does he find rest—such rest as may come to him. In truth he is a leader among his race — one of those silent but powerful influences which, building broadly and at the base, are making up a reconstructed South.

Leveridge is out in the West, as cheerfully as he may, practicing law.

Barnard is also out of the army, and fills, ably and honorably, an office in the state government of New York.

Oakland may be seen at five o'clock of most any afternoon coming from his business up Broadway. He has his own love affair, but that does not come into our story.

These men, who served their country so nobly on the battle-field, are examples of that marvelous incident in our national history where a million of men have, as it were, in a day passed from a life which outrages every principle of social order, and have become absorbed in our peaceful community as the snow-flake falls into the bosom of the placid river.

Harold Dalton is prosperously engaged in business in Savannah. He sees every day the men who but a little while ago were his bitter persecutors. Have they repented for those cruel outrages? Has Harold forgiven them?

A few days ago we saw Colonel Dalton and his wife at the Exhibition of the Academy of Design. They were happy as two flowers are happy that grow upon the same stalk. They stood before a powerfully painted picture entitled "The Sanctuary."

"Horton and I were near by at the time that incident occurred," said Dalton; "and when the group of refugees and negroes which he has so graphically portrayed came in sight of the old flag on the fort, and fell upon their knees in prayer, it seemed to me that the scene was emblematical, and that beneath the folds of our national banner we could say, without a blush, that there was not only liberty and safety for the freed black, but that it was the SANCTUARY for the oppressed of all the world.

BY MISS MULOCK.

These novels form a most admirable series of popular fiction. They are marked by their faithful delineation of character, their naturalness and purity of sentiment, the dramatic interest of their plots, their beauty and force of expression, and their elevated moral tone. No current novels can be more highly recommended for the family library, while their brilliancy and vivacity will make them welcome to every reader of cultivated taste.

A NOBLE LIFE. 12mo, Cloth, $1 50.

CHRISTIAN'S MISTAKE. 12mo, Cloth, $1 50.

JOHN HALIFAX, GENTLEMAN. 8vo, Paper, 75 cents; Library Edition, 12mo, Cloth, $1 50.

A LIFE FOR A LIFE. 8vo, Paper, 50 cents; Library Edition, 12mo, Cloth, $1 50.

A HERO, AND OTHER TALES. A Hero, Bread upon the Waters, and Alice Learmont. 12mo, Cloth, $1 25.

AGATHA'S HUSBAND. 8vo, Paper, 50 cents.

AVILLION, AND OTHER TALES. 8vo, Paper, $1 25.

OLIVE. 8vo, Paper, 50 cents.

THE FAIRY BOOK. The Best popular Fairy Stories selected and rendered anew. Engravings. 16mo, Cloth, $1 50.

THE HEAD OF THE FAMILY. 8vo, Paper, 75 cents.

MISTRESS AND MAID. A Household Story. 8vo, Paper, 50 cents.

NOTHING NEW. Tales. 8vo, Paper, 50 cents.

THE OGILVIES. 8vo, Paper, 50 cents.

OUR YEAR: A Child's Book in Prose and Verse. Illustrated by CLARENCE DOBELL. 16mo, Cloth, gilt edges, $1 00.

STUDIES FROM LIFE. 12mo, Cloth, gilt edges, $1 00.

PUBLISHED BY HARPER & BROTHERS, NEW YORK.

☞ Sent by Mail, postage free, to any part of the United States, on receipt of the price.

BY GEORGE ELIOT.

ADAM BEDE. 12mo, Cloth, $1 50.

FELIX HOLT, THE RADICAL. 8vo, Paper, 75 cents.
  A Library Edition, 12mo, Cloth, $2 00.

THE MILL ON THE FLOSS. 12mo, Cloth, $1 50; 8vo, Paper, 75 cents.

ROMOLA. With Illustrations. 8vo, Cloth, $2 00; Paper, $1 50.

SCENES OF CLERICAL LIFE. 8vo, Paper, 75 cents.

SILAS MARNER, THE WEAVER OF RAVELOE. 12mo, Cloth, $1 50.

It was once said of a very charming and high-minded woman that to know her was in itself a liberal education; and we are inclined to set an almost equally high value on an acquaintance with the writings of "George Eliot." For those who read them aright they possess the faculty of educating in its highest sense, of invigorating the intellect, giving a healthy tone to the taste, appealing to the nobler feelings of the heart, training its impulses aright, and awakening or developing in every mind the consciousness of a craving for something higher than the pleasures and rewards of that life which only the senses realize, the belief in a destiny of a nobler nature than can be grasped by experience or demonstrated by argument. On those readers who are able to appreciate a lofty independence of thought, a rare nobility of feeling, and an exquisite sympathy with the joys and sorrows of human nature, "George Eliot's" writings can not fail to exert an invigorating and purifying influence, the good effects of which leaves behind it a lasting impression.—*London Review*.

"George Eliot," or whoever he or she may be, has a wonderful power in giving an air of intense reality to whatever scene is presented, whatever character is portrayed.—*Worcester Palladium*.

She resembles Shakspeare in her power of delineation. It is from this characteristic action on the part of each of the members of the *dramatis personæ* that we feel not only an interest, even and consistent throughout, but also an admiration for "George Eliot" above all other writers.—*Philadelphia Evening Telegraph*.

Few women—no living woman indeed—have so much strength as "George Eliot," and, more than that, she never allows it to degenerate into coarseness. With all her so-called "masculine" vigor, she has a feminine tenderness, which is nowhere shown more plainly than in her descriptions of children.—*Boston Transcript*.

She looks out upon the world with the most entire enjoyment of all the good that there is in it to enjoy, and with an enlarged compassion for all the ill that there is in it to pity. But she never either whimpers over the sorrowful lot of man, or snarls and chuckles over his follies and littlenesses and impotence.—*Saturday Review*.

Her acquaintance with different phases of outward life, and the power of analyzing feeling and the working of the mind, are alike wonderful.—*Reader*.

"George Eliot's" novels belong to the enduring literature of our country—durable, not for the fashionableness of its pattern, but for the texture of its stuff.—*Examiner*.

PUBLISHED BY HARPER & BROTHERS, NEW YORK.

HARPER & BROTHERS *will send any of the above works by Mail, postage prepaid, to any part of the United States, on receipt of the price.*

www.ingramcontent.com/pod-product-compliance
Lightning Source LLC
Chambersburg PA
CBHW032119230426
43672CB00009B/1796